Narada

A Manual of Buddhism

Publication of the Buddhist Missionary Society
Buddhist Vihara,
123, Jalan Berhala,
50470, Kuala Lumpur, Malaysia.

Cover design by Chong Hong Choo
Typeset by Sykt. Broadway Typesetting Sdn. Bhd.
Printed by Sykt. Percetakan & Perniagaan Acme
Lithography by Photo Litho K.L.

ISBN 967-9920-58-5

CONTENTS

ABOUT THIS BOOK

This is a fairly comprehensive book enabling the reader to appreciate and understand certain important finer aspects of Thēravāda Buddhism. This book would also serve as a reference, for both Teachers and Students alike, gain a good insight into the fundamentals of Buddhism.

The author, the late Venerable Nārada Mahā Thera was a well-known Buddhist Missioner. He is also the author of many other Buddhist Publications. We are grateful to him for his kind permission, enabling this reprint to be effected in Malaysia.

Special thanks are due to Ven. U. Nipuna Mr. Tan Teik Beng, Mr. Eddy Yu Chen Lim, Ms. Quah Pin Pin and Ms. Chong Hong Choo for their valuable assistance in the reproduction of this book.

K. SRI DHAMMANANDA J.S.M.

Buddhist Missionary Society
Buddhist Vihara, Jalan Berhala,
50470 Kuala Lumpur, Malaysia
September, 1992

1 THE LIFE OF THE BUDDHA

The Birth

On the full-moon day of May[1] in the year 623 B.C.,[2] there was born, in the Lumbini Park[3] at Kapilavatthu,[4] on the borders of Nepal, a noble Prince of aristocratic Sākya clan. His father was King Suddhōdana,[5] and his mother Queen Mahā Māyā. Seven days after the birth of the child, the mother died, and Mahā Pajāpati Gōtami, her younger sister, who was also married to King Suddhōdana, became his fostermother.

Great were the rejoicings of the people over the birth of this illustrious prince. A certain ascetic, named Asita, also known as Kāladēvala, was particularly pleased to hear this happy news and, being a tutor of the King, visited the palace to see the royal baby. The overjoyed King brought the child, to pay him due reverence, but, to the surprise of all, his feet turned and planted them-selves in the matted locks of the ascetic. Instantly the ascetic rose from his seat and foreseeing the child's future greatness, saluted him with joined hands. When he thus honored him, the royal father too saluted him in the same way.

The great ascetic at first smiled and then was

sad. Questioned as to his mixed feelings, he replied that he smiled because the Prince would, eventually become a Buddha; and that he was sad because he, owing to his prior death and rebirth in a *Formless Plane – Arūpalōka,*[6] could not benefit by the superior wisdom of the Enlightened One.

The Naming Ceremony

On the fifth day after the Prince's birth, he was named Siddhattha Gōtama, which means 'wishfulfilled'. His family name was Gōtama.[7]

In accordance with the ancient custom, many learned Brahmins were invited to the palace for this naming ceremony. Amongst them were eight distinguished men. Examining the characteristics of the child, seven of them raised two fingers and gave a double interpretation, saying that he would either become a Universal Monarch or a Buddha. But the youngest Kondañña, who excelled the others in knowledge, raised only one finger and firmly declared that he would definitely retire from the world and become a Buddha.

The Ploughing Festival

A very remarkable incident took place in his childhood. It was an unprecedented mental experience which, in later life, during his search after Truth, served as a key to his Enlightenment.

As an encouragement to agriculture the King arranged for a Ploughing Festival. It was indeed a festive occasion for all, as both nobles and commoners decked in gala dress participated in the ceremony. On the appointed day the King, accompanied by his courtiers, went to the field taking with him, the young Prince together with the nurses. Placing the child on a screened and canopied couch under the cool shade of a rose-apple tree to be watched by the nurses, the King took an active part in the Ploughing Festival. When the festival was at its climax, the nurses stole away from the Prince's presence to catch a glimpse of the wonderful spectacle. The thoughtful child, mature in intellect though young in age, seeing none by him, sat cross-legged, and intently concentrating on inhalation and exhalation, gained one-pointedness of the mind and developed the First Ecstasy – *Jhāna*.[8]

In the midst of their enjoyment the neglectful nurses suddenly remembered their duty, and when they saw the Prince absorbed in meditation, were struck with awe and immediately reported the matter to the King. He hastened to the scene and beholding the Prince in meditative posture, saluted him saying: "This, dear child is my second salutation."

Prince Siddhattha's Youth

As a royal child Prince Siddhattha no doubt received a good education, although the books give no details about his schooling. Being a scion of the warrior race, he must have been specially trained in the art of warfare.

At the early age of sixteen, he married his

beautiful cousin Princess Yasōdharā,[9] who was of equal years. After his happy marriage, he led a luxurious life, blissfully unaware of the vicissitudes of life, outside the palace gates.

Of his luxurious life as a prince he states:–
"I was delicate, excessively delicate. In my father's dwelling three lotus ponds were made purposely for me. Blue lotuses bloomed in one, red in another, and white in the third. I used no sandalwood that was not of Kāsi.[10] My turban, tunic, dress and cloak were all from Kāsi. Night and day a white parasol was held over me so that I might not be touched by heat or cold, dust, leaves or dew."

"There were three palaces built for me – one for the cold season, one for the hot season, one for the rainy season. During the four rainy months, I lived in the palace for the rainy season, entertained by female musicians, without coming down from the palace. Just as in the houses of others, food from the husks of rice together with sour gruel is given to the slaves and workmen, even so, in my father's dwelling, food with rice and meat was given to the slaves and workmen".

Renunciation

With the march of time truth gradually dawned upon him. His contemplative nature and boundless compassion did not permit him to enjoy the fleeting pleasures of a royal household. He knew no woe, but he felt deep pity for sorrowing humanity. Amidst comfort and prosperity he realized the universality of sorrow.

One glorious day, as he went out of the palace to see the world outside, he came into direct contact with the stark realities of life. Within the narrow confines of the palaces, he saw only the rosy side of life; but the dark side, the common lot of mankind was veiled from him. His observant eyes met the strange sight of a decrepit old man, a diseased person, a corpse, and a dignified hermit. The first three sights convinced him of the inexorable nature of life and the universal sickness of humanity. The fourth signified the means to overcome the ills of life and attain calm and peace.

Realizing the worthlessness of sensual pleasures highly prized by ordinary men, and the value of renunciation in which the wise seek delight, he decided to leave the world in search of Truth and Peace.

When this final decision was made after much deliberation, the seemingly happy news of the birth of a son was conveyed to him. Contrary to expectation he was not overjoyed but regarded the first and only offspring as an impediment. Normally an ordinary father would have welcomed the joyful tidings, but Prince Siddhattha, extra-ordinary father as he was, exclaimed, "An impediment – *rāhu,* has been born; a fetter has arisen". The infant son was accordingly named *Rāhula* by his grandfather.

The palace was no longer a congenial place for the destined Buddha. The time was ripe for him to depart.

He ordered his favourite charioteer Channa to saddle the horse Kanthaka, and went to the suite of apartments occupied by the Princess. Opening the door of the chamber, he stood on the threshold and cast his dispassionate glance on the wife and child who were fast asleep. His compassion for his two dear ones as well as for the whole world dominated him at the moment of parting. He was not worried about the future worldly comforts and happinesses of the mother and child as they had everything in abundance and were well protected.

Leaving all behind with a light heart, he stole away from the palace at midnight and rode into the dark on his horse, attended only by his loyal charioteer. As a penniless wanderer he went forth in search of Truth and Peace.

It was in his twenty-ninth year, the turning-point of his career, that Prince Siddhattha made this historic journey.

He journeyed far, and crossing the river Anomā, rested on the bank. Here he shaved his hair and beard and, handing over his garments and ornaments to Channa with instructions to return to the palace, adopted the simple yellow garb of an ascetic and led a life of voluntary poverty.

The ascetic Siddhattha, who as a Prince had lived in the lap of luxury, became a penniless and homeless wanderer living on what little the charitable gave of their own accord.

He had no permanent abode. A shady tree or a lonely cave sheltered him day and night. Barefooted and bareheaded, he walked in the

PRINCE SIDDHATTHA'S GENEALOGICAL TABLE

Father's Side

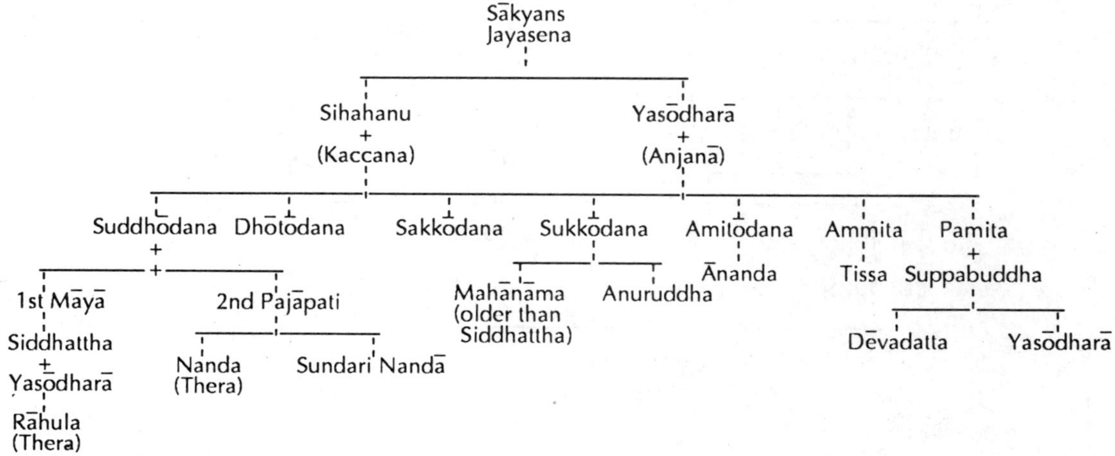

Mother's Side

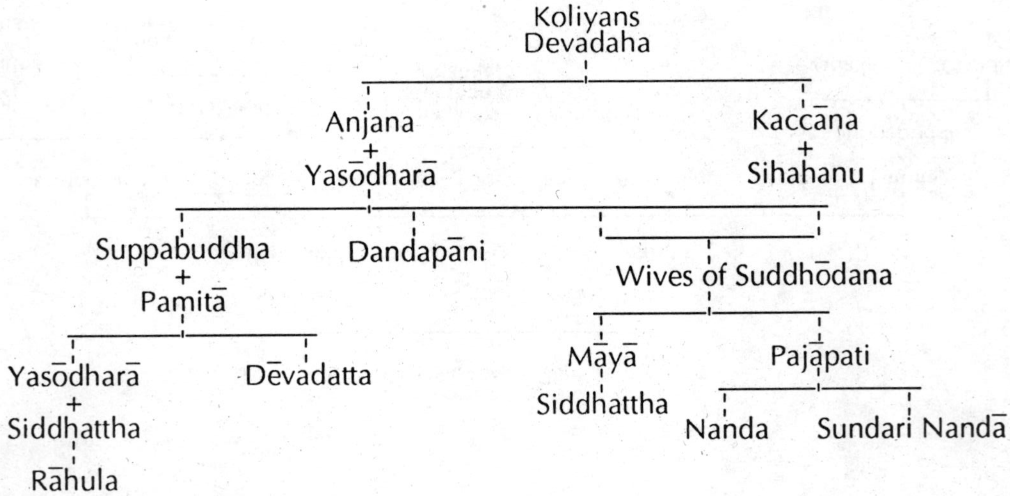

scorching sun and in the piercing cold. His humble dress was made of cast-off, worthless, coarse rags. With no possession to call his own except a bowl to collect his food and robes just sufficient to cover the body, he concentrated all his time and energies upon discovering the Truth.

The Search

As a seeker after what is good (*kim kusalagavēsi*) searching for the unsurpassed peaceful state most excellent, he approached Ālāra Kālāma an ascetic of repute, and speedily learnt his doctrine and developed the seventh Arūpa Jhāna, the Realm of Nothingness, (*Ākincaññāyatana*), an advanced stage of concentration.

The unenvious teacher, delighted to hear of the success of his distinguished pupil, honoured him by placing him on a level with himself and admiringly said:–

"Happy, friend, are we; yea, extremely happy, in that we look up to a respected ascetic like you! The doctrine which I know, that also do you know; and the doctrine which you know, that I know also. As I am, so are you; as you are, so am I. Come, friend, let both of us lead the company of ascetics."

The ascetic Gōtama was not satisfied with mere mental concentration and an ordinary system, which did not lead to Nibbāna. Dissatisfied with Kālāma's system, he left him, and approached one Uddakā Rāmaputta, who readily admitted him as a pupil.

Before long the intelligent ascetic Gōtama

mastered his doctrine and attained the final stage of mental concentration, The Realm of Neither *Perception nor Non-perception – Nēva saññā nāsaññāyatana.* This is the highest stage in worldly concentration when conciousness becomes so subtle and refined that it cannot be said that a consciousness either exists or not. Ancient sages could not proceed any further in mental development.

His teacher then honoured the ascetic Gōtama further by inviting him to take full charge of all disciples as their teacher. He said:–

"Happy, friend , are we; yea, extremely happy in that we see such a venerable ascetic as you! The doctrine which Rāma knew, you know; the doctrine which you know, Rāma knew. As was Rāma, so are you; as you are, so was Rāma. Come, friend, henceforth you shall lead this company of ascetics."

Still he felt that his quest of life was not achieved. He was seeking Nibbāna, the complete cessation of suffering. Dissatisfied with Rāmaputta's system too, he departed.

He found that nobody was competent to teach him what he sought as all were enmeshed in ignorance. He gave up seeking external help, for Truth and Peace are to be found within.

His Struggle for Enlightenment

Meeting with disappointment but not discouraged, the ascetic Gōtama, seeking for the incomparable state of Peace Supreme, wandered in the district of

Magadha and arrived in due course at Uruvela, the market town of Sēnāni. There he spied a lovely spot of ground, a charming forest grove, a flowing river with pleasant sandy fords, and near by was a village where he could beg for his food.

The place was congenial for his meditation. The atmosphere was peaceful, the surroundings were pleasant, the scenery charming. He resolved to settle down there alone to achieve his desired object.

Hearing of his renunciation Kondañña, the youngest Brahmin who predicted his future, and four sons of the other sages – *Bhaddiya, Vappa, Mahānāma,* and *Assaji* – also renounced the world, and joined his company.

In ancient India great importance was attached to rites, ceremonies, penances, and sacrifices. It was then a popular belief that no salvation could be gained unless one led a life of strict asceticism. Accordingly for six long years he made a superhuman struggle practising all forms of severe austerity, with the result that his delicate body was reduced almost to a skeleton. The more he tormented his body, the farther his goal receded from him.

Temptation of Māra the Evil One

His prolonged painful austerities proved utterly futile. They only resulted in the exhaustion of his energy. Though physically a superman, on account of his delicate nurture as a prince, he could not possibly stand the great strain. His graceful form faded almost beyond recognition. His golden-coloured skin turned pale, blood dried up, sinews and muscles shrivelled, his eyes were sunk and blurred.

At this critical stage, Māra[11] approached the ascetic Gōtama and said:–

"You are lean and deformed. Near to you is death. A thousand parts (of you belong) to death; to life (there remains) but one. Live, O good sir; life is better. Living you could perform merit. By leading a life of celibacy and making fire sacrifices, much merit could be acquired. What will you do with this striving? Hard is the path of striving, difficult and not easily accomplished."

He replied:–

"O Evil One, kinsman of the heedless! You have come here for your own sake. Even an iota of merit is of no avail. To them who are in need of merit it behoves you, Māra, to speak thus. *Confidence – Saddhā, self-control – Tapo, energy – Viriya, and wisdom – Paññā* are mine. Why do you question me, who am thus intent, about life?"

"Even the streams of rivers will this wind dry up. Why should not the blood of one who is thus striving dry up? When the blood dries up, the bile and phlegm also dry up. When my flesh wastes away, more and more does my mind get clarified. Still more do my mindfulness, wisdom, and concentration become firm."

"While I live thus, experiencing the utmost pain, my mind does not long for lust. Behold the purity of a being!"

Sense-desires – Kāma, are your first enemy,

The second is called *Aversion – Ārati,*
The third is *Hunger* and *Thirst – Khuppipāsa,*
The fourth is called *Craving – Tanhā,*
The fifth is *Sloth* and *Torpor – Thina-Middha,*
The sixth is called *Fear – Bhaya,*
The seventh is *Doubt – Vicikicchā,* and
The eighth is *Detraction* and *Obstinacy – Makkha-Thambha,*
The ninth is *Profit – Lābha, Praise – Silōka,*
Honour – Sakkāra, and that ill-gotten *Fame –Yąsa.*
The tenth is the extolling of oneself and the contempt of others.

"This is your army, the opposing host of the Evil One. That army the coward does not overcome, but he who overcomes obtains happiness."

"This Munja[12] do I display! What boots life in this world! Better for me is death in the battle than that one should live on, vanquished!".

With these words the ascetic Gōtama dismissed Māra and made a firm determination to attain his goal, Buddhahood.

The Middle Path

The ascetic Gōtama was now fully convinced, through personal experience, of the utter futility of self-mortification. Abandoning it forever, he adopted an independent course – *the Majjhimā Patipadā – the Middle Path.*

He recalled how when his father was engaged in ploughing, he sat in the cool shade of the rose-apple tree, having attained to the first Ecstasy. He thought – well, this is the Path to Enlightenment!

He realized that Enlightenment could not be gained with an exhausted body. So he decided to take some food. The five ascetics who attended on him, disappointed at this unexpected change of method, deserted him and went to Isipatana, saying that "the ascetic Gōtama had become indulgent, had ceased from striving, and had returned to a life of comfort."

At a crucial time when help would have been most welcome, his only companions left him, but he was not discouraged.

After a substantial meal offered by Sujātā, a generous lady, he made a firm resolve not to rise from his seat until he attained Buddhahood.

The Enlightenment

One happy Vesak night, as he was seated under the famous Pippala[13] tree at Buddha Gayā, with mind tranquilized and purified, in the first watch he developed that supernormal knowledge which enabled him to remember his past lives *Pubbenivāsānussati Ñāna – Reminiscence of Past Births.* In the middle watch he developed the clairvoyant supernormal vision dealing with the death and rebirth of beings *Cutūpapāta Ñāna – Perception of the Disappearing and Reappearing of Beings.*

In the last watch of the night he developed the supernormal knowledge with regard to the *destruction of passions – Āsavakkhaya Ñāna,* and comprehending things as they truly are, attained *Perfect Enlightenment*[14] *– Sammā Sambōdhi.*

Having in his 35th year attained Buddhahood, that supreme state of Perfection, He devoted the remainder of that precious life to serve humanity both by example and precept, dominated by no personal motive.

The Buddha was a human being. As a man He was born, as a man He lived, and as a man His life came to an end. Though human, He became *an extraordinary man – Acchariya Manussa.* The Buddha laid stress on this fact and left no room for anyone to fall into the error of thinking that He was an immortal being. There is no deification in the case of the Buddha.

Nor does the Buddha claim to be an incarnation of Vishnu, nor does He call himself a "Saviour" who freely saves others by His personal salvation. The Buddha exhorts His disciples to depend on themselves for their salvation, for both defilement and purity depend on oneself. "You yourselves should make the exertion. The Tathāgatas are only teachers," says the Buddha.

The Buddhas point out the path, and it is left for us to follow that path to save ourselves.

"To depend on others for salvation is negative, but to depend on oneself is positive." Dependence on others means a surrender of one's effort.

Furthermore, the Buddha does not claim a monopoly of Buddhahood, which as matter of fact is not the prerogative of any specially graced, chosen person. He reached the highest possible state of perfection any person could aspire to; and without the closed fist of a teacher, He revealed the only straight path that leads thereto. According to the teachings of the Buddha anybody may aspire to that supreme state of perfection if he makes the necessary aspiring determination and necessary exertion.

As a man He attained Buddhahood and proclaimed to the world the latent possibilities and the creative power of man. Instead of placing an unseen almighty God over man, and making him subservient to such a belief, He raised the worth of mankind. It was He who taught that man could obtain his Deliverance from sorrow by his own exertion, without depending on a God and mediating priests, or on sacrifices and prayers. It was He who taught the ego-centric world the noble ideal of selfless service. It was He who revolted against the degrading caste system and taught the equality of mankind. He declared that the gates of success and prosperity were open to all, in every condition of life, high and low, saint and sinner, who would care to turn over a new leaf and aspire to Perfection.

Irrespective of caste, colour or rank, he established for both deserving men and women a celibate order which was "democratic in constitution and communistic in distribution". He gave complete freedom of thought and wanted us to open our eyes to see things as they truly are. He comforted the bereaved by His consoling words. He ministered to the sick that were deserted. He helped the poor who were neglected. He ennobled the lives of sinners and purified the corrupted lives of criminals. He encouraged the feeble, united the divided, enlightened the ignorant, clarified the mystic, guided the deluded, elevated the base, and dignified the noble. Rich and poor, saint and sinner, loved Him alike. Despotic and righteous kings, glorious and obscure princes and nobles, generous and miserly millionaires, haughty and humble scholars, destitute paupers, downtrodden scavengers, wicked murderers, despised courtesans – all benefited by His words of wisdom and compassion.

His noble example was a source of inspiration to all. His Message of Peace was hailed by all with indescribable joy, and was of eternal benefit to everyone who had the fortune to come under its benign influence.

2 SOON AFTER THE ENLIGHTENMENT

A Paean of Joy – *Udāna Gāthā*

THRO' many a birth in *Sansāra*[1] wandered I,
Seeking but not finding, the builder[2] of this house.
Sorrowful is repeated birth.
O house-builder! Thou art seen.
Thou shalt build no house[3] again,
All thy rafters[4] are broken,
thy ridge-pole[5] is shattered.
The Mind attains the Unconditioned.[6]
Achieved is the End of Craving.

Dhammapada vv. 153, 154

The Seven Weeks after the Enlightenment

On the auspicious day preceding the Enlightenment, the Bōdhisatta[7] ate some milk-porridge offered by a generous lady named Sujātā. After the Enlightenment for seven weeks the Buddha fasted, and spent His time under the Bōdhi tree and in its neighbourhood.

The whole of the first week the Buddha sat under the Bōdhi tree in one posture, experiencing the *Bliss of Emancipation – Vimutti Sukha.*

At the end of the seven days the Buddha

emerged from that state of concentration, and in the first watch of the night[8] thoroughly reflected on *Dependent Arising – Paticca Samuppāda,* in direct order thus: When this (cause) exists, this (effect) is; with the arising of this (cause), this (effect) arises.

In the middle watch of the night[9] the Buddha thoroughly reflected on "Dependent Arising" in reverse order thus:–

"When this (cause) does not exist, this (effect) is not; with the cessation of this (cause), this (effect) ceases."

In the third watch of the night the Buddha reflected on "Dependent Arising" in direct and reverse order thus:–

"When this (cause) exists, this (effect) is, with the arising of this (cause) this (effect) arises; when this (cause) does not exist this (effect) is not; with the cessation of this (cause), this (effect) ceases."

Throughout the second week, as a mark of gratitude to the Bōdhi tree that sheltered Him during His struggle for Enlightenment, the Buddha stood gazing at it with motionless eyes.[10]

During the third week the Buddha paced up and down on a *jewelled promenade – Ratana Cankamana* near the Bōdhi tree.

The fourth week He spent in a *jewelled chamber*[11] – *Ratanāghara* meditating on the Abhidhamma.

During the fifth week He dwelt under the Ajapāla Banyan tree in the vicinity of the Bōdhi tree. Here the Buddha sat in one posture for seven days enjoying this Bliss of Emancipation. When He emerged from that state of concentration, a certain conceited Brahmin approached the Buddha and questioned Him thus:–

"In what respect, O Venerable Gōtama, does one become a Brahmin, and what are the conditions that make a Brahmin?"

Then the Blessed One uttered this paean of joy:–

"That Brahmin who has discarded evil, without *conceit – huhunka,* free from defilements, self-controlled, versed in knowledge, who has led the Holy Life – rightly would call himself a Brahmin. For him there is no elation anywhere in this world."

According to the Jātaka Commentary it was during His stay at the foot of this tree that the three daughters[12] of Māra – Tanhā, Arati, and Rāga – came to tempt the Buddha.

From the Ajapāla Banyan tree the Buddha proceeded to the Mucalinda tree where He spent the sixth week. Here, too, the Buddha sat for seven days enjoying the Bliss of Emancipation. At that time there arose an unexpected great shower. Rain and gloomy weather with cold winds prevailed for seven days.

Thereupon Mucalinda, the serpent-king,[13] came out of his abode and coiling round the body of the Blessed One seven times, remained keeping his large hood over the head of the Blessed One so that the Blessed One may not be touched by cold, heat, gadflies, gnats, wind, sun or reptiles.

At the close of seven days Mucalinda seeing the clear, cloudless sky, uncoiled himself from around the body of the Blessed One, and leaving his own form, took the guise of a young man, and stood in front of the Blessed One with joined hands.

Thereupon the Buddha uttered this paean of joy:–

"Happy is seclusion to him who is contented, to him who has heard the Truth, and to him who sees. Happy is goodwill in this world, and so is restraint towards all beings. Happy in this world, is non-attachment, the passing beyond sense-desires. The suppression of the 'I am' conceit is indeed the highest happiness."

The seventh week the Buddha spent at the Rājāyatana tree. Here too the Buddha sat in one posture for seven days enjoying the Bliss of Emancipation.

The First Two Converts

At that time two merchants, Tapassu and Bhalluka, from Ukkalā (Orissā) were travelling to their native town. Then a Dēvatā[14] who was a blood-relative of these two merchants, spoke to them as follows:–

"The Blessed One, good sirs, is dwelling at the foot of the Rājāyatana tree, soon after His Enlightenment. Go and serve the Blessed One with flour and honeycomb. It will conduce to your well-being and happiness for a long time."

Thereupon the two merchants, Tapassu and Bhalluka, took with them flour and honeycomb, and approaching the Buddha said:–

"O Lord, may the Blessed One accept this flour

and honeycomb so that it may long tend to our well-being and happiness!"

Then it occurred to the Blessed One:–

"The Tathāgatas do not accept food with their hands. How shall I accept this flour and honeycomb?"

Forthwith the four Great Kings[15] understood the thoughts of the Blessed One and from the four directions offered Him four stone bowls,[16] saying:–

"O Lord, may the Blessed One accept in these the flour and honeycomb!"

The Blessed One accepted the new bowls, received the flour and honeycomb in them, and ate thereof.

When the Buddha finished His meal the two merchants prostrated themselves before His feet and said:–

"We, O Lord, seek refuge in the Buddha and the Dhamma. May the Blessed One treat us as lay disciples who have sought refuge from today till death!"

They were the first disciples who took the twofold formula.[17]

3 THE BUDDHA PROPOUNDS HIS DHAMMA

Invitation to teach the Dhamma

AT the close of the fasting period, as the Buddha was engaged in solitary meditation, He thought:–

"With difficulty have I apprehended the Dhamma. There is no need to proclaim it now. This Dhamma is not easily understood by those who are overcome by lust and hatred. The lust-ridden, shrouded by the mass darkness, do not see this Dhamma, which goes against the stream, abstruse, profound, difficult to perceive, and subtle."

Eventually His mind turned into inaction, and not to the teaching of the Dhamma.

Thereupon a celestial being named Brahma Sahampati read the thoughts of the Blessed One, and fearing that the world might perish through not hearing the Dhamma, approached the Buddha and invited Him to teach the Dhamma.

He wisely remarked:–

"In ancient times there arose in Magadha a Dhamma, impure, evolved by the corrupted. Open this Door to the Deathless. May they hear the

Dhamma, understood by the Stainless! Just as one standing on the summit of a rocky mountain would behold the people around, even so may the All-Seeing Wise One ascend this palace of Dhamma! May the Sorrowless One look upon the people, plunged in grief and overcome by birth and decay."

"Rise, O Hero, the victor in battle, the caravan-leader, the debt-free One, and wander in the world! May the Blessed One propound the Dhamma! There will be those who will understand the Doctrine!"

When Brahma Sahampati entreated the Buddha for the third time, He surveyed the world with His Buddha Vision.

On surveying the world[1] He perceived beings with little as well as much dust in their eyes, with keen and dull intellect, with good and bad characteristics, who are easy and difficult to be taught, and a few others who live perceiving the dangers of evil and of a future life.

The Buddha, therefore, accepted the invitation of Brahma Sahampati and said:–

"Opened to them are the Doors to the Deathless.[2] Let those who have ears repose confidence. Being aware of the weariness of it, O Brahma, I did not preach amongst men this glorious and excellent Dhamma."

The delighted Brahma, thinking – "I made myself the occasion for the Blessed One to expound the Dhamma," respectfully saluted Him and straightaway disappeared.

On the Way to Benares to Teach the Dhamma
"To whom shall I teach the Dhamma first? Who will understand the Dhamma quickly?" was the first thought that occurred to the Buddha before He embarked on His noble Mission.

"Well, there is Ālāra Kālāma,[3] who is learned, clever, wise, and has for long been with little dust in his eyes. How if I were to teach the Dhamma to him first? He will understand the Dhamma quickly."

Then a deity appeared before the Blessed One and said:–

"Lord! Ālāra Kālāma died a week ago." With His Divine Eye He perceived that it was so. Then He thought of Uddakā Rāmaputta.[4] Instantly a deity informed Him that he died the evening before. With His Divine Eye the Buddha perceived this to be true.

Ultimately He thought of the five Bhikkhus who attended on Him during His struggle for Enlightenment. With His superhuman Divine Eye He perceived that they were residing in the Deer Park at Isipatana in Benares. So the Buddha stayed at Uruvela as long as He wished and set out for Benares.

Between Gayā and the Bodhi,[5] Upaka, a wandering ascetic, saw the Buddha travelling on the highway, and said:–

"Extremely clear are your senses, friend! Pure and clean is your complexion. On account of whom have you renounced, friend? Who is your teacher? Whose doctrine do you profess?"

The Buddha replied:–

"All have I overcome, all do I know.
From all am I detached, all have I renounced.
Wholly absorbed am I in the
destruction of craving (Arahantship)
Having comprehended all by myself
who shall I call my teacher?
No teacher have I[6]
An equal to me there is not.
In the world, including the gods,
there is no rival to me.
Indeed an Arahant am I in this world.
An unsurpassed teacher am I.
Alone am I the All-Enlightened.
Cool and appeased am I.
To establish the wheel of Dhamma I
go to the city of kāsi
In this blind world
I shall beat the drum of Deathlessness."

"Then, friend, you do admit that you are an Arahant, a limitless Conqueror?" queried Upaka.

"Like me are conquerors who have attained to the destruction of Defilements. All the evil conditions have I conquered. Hence, Upaka, I am called a Conqueror," replied the Buddha.

" It may be so, friend!" Upaka curtly remarked, and nodding his head, turned into a by-road and departed.

Unperturbed by the first rebuff the Buddha

received, He wandered from place to place and arrived in due course at the Deer Park in Benares.

The five monks who saw Him coming from a far resolved not to pay him due respect as they misconstrued His change of effort during His struggle for Enlightenment. But as the Buddha drew near, His august personality was such that they were compelled to receive Him with due honour. Nevertheless, they addressed Him by name and by the title 'Āvuso' (friend) a form of address applied generally to juniors. The Blessed One advised them not to address Him thus as He had attained Buddhahood. But the sceptical monks refused to believe Him. For the second and third time the Buddha advised them. Yet the monks refused to acknowledge His superiority.

Finally the Buddha said:–

"Do you know, O Bhikkhus, of an occasion when I ever spoke to you thus before?"

"Nay, indeed, Lord!"

"The Tathāgata, O Bhikkhus, is not luxurious, has not given up striving, and has not adopted a life of abundance. An Exalted One, O Bhikkhus, is the the Tathāgata: a Fully Enlightened One is He. Give ear, O Bhikkhus! Immortality has been attained. I shall instruct and teach the Dhamma. If you act according to my instructions, you will before long realize, by your own intuitive wisdom, and thereafter continue attaining in this life itself, that supreme state of the Holy Life, for the sake of which sons of noble families rightly renounce the household for the homeless life."

It was a frank utterance, issuing from the sacred mouth of the Buddha. The cultured monks, though adamant in their views, were now fully convinced of the great achievement of the Buddha and of His competence to act as their spiritual Guide.

Two of the Bhikkhus the Buddha instructed, whilst three went out for alms. With what they brought, all the six sustained themselves. Three of the Bhikkhus He instructed, whilst two Bhikkhus went out for alms. With what they brought, all the six sustained themselves.

The *Dhammacakkappavattana Sutta* was the first discourse the Buddha delivered to them. Hearing it Kondañña, the eldest, attained *Sōtāpatti,* the first stage of Sainthood. The other four attained Sōtāpatti later. It was after hearing the *Anattalakkhana* Sutta, which deals with soullessness, that they all attained Arahantship, the final stage of Sainthood.

The Five Monks

The five Bhikkhus who thus attained Arahantship and became His first disciples were Kondañña, Bhaddiya, Vappa, Mahānāma and Assaji.

Kondañña was the youngest of the eight Brahmins invited for the naming ceremony, and who alone foretold that the prince would definitely become the Buddha. The other four disciples were sons of four of the other seven Brahmins. These five Brahmins had retired to the forest as ascetics in anticipation of the renunciation of Prince Siddhattha, and at Uruvela they had attended on him when he was striving to attain Buddhahood. But when he gave up fasting and penance, they left him and went to Isipatana. Soon after their departure, he attained Buddhahood. It was seven weeks after His Enlightenment that the Buddha visited Isipatana and expounded the doctrine to them.

The Venerable Kondañña became the first Arahant and the senior member of the Sangha. It was the Venerable Assaji, one of the five, who converted the great Sāriputta, the first chief disciple of the Buddha.

4 THE FIRST DISCOURSE

DHAMMACAKKAPPAVATTANA SUTTA[1]

THUS have I heard:-

On one occasion the Blessed One was residing at the Deer Park[2] in Isipatana, near Benares. Thereupon the Blessed One addressed the five Bhikkhus as follows:–

"There are two extreme (*Anta*) which should be avoided by a recluse."

"(The) constant attachment to *Sensual Pleasures*[3] – *Kāmasukhallikānuyōga* which is base, vulgar, worldly, ignoble, and profitless; and (the) constant addiction to *Self-Mortifi-Cation*[4] – *Attakilamathānuyōga* which is a painful ignoble, and profitless.[5]"

"Avoiding these two extremes, O Bhikkhus, the Tathāgata has discovered the *Middle Path – Majjhimā Patipadā* which promotes sight, knowledge, *Peace – Vupasamaya, Higher Wisdom – Abhiññāya, Enlightenment – Sambōdhāya, and Nibbānāya.*"

"What, O Bhikkhus, is that Middle Path the Tathāgata has discovered which promotes sight, knowledge, peace, Higher Wisdom, Enlightenment, and Nibbāna?"

"It is this **Noble Eightfold Path** – namely, *Right Understanding – Sammā Ditthi, Right Thoughts– Sammā Sankappa, Right Speech – Sammā Vācā, Right Action – Sammā Kammanta, Right Livelihood – Sammā Ājīva, Right Effort – Sammā Vāyāma, Right Mindfulness–Sammā Sati, and Right Concentration – Sammā Samādhi.* This, O Bhikkhus, is the Middle Path which the Tathāgata has found out."

(1) "Now this, O Bhikkhus, is The Noble Truth of suffering:– Birth is suffering, decay is suffering, disease is suffering, death is suffering, to be united with the unpleasant is suffering, to be separated from the pleasant is suffering, not to receive what one desires is suffering, in brief, the five Aggregates of Attachment[6] are suffering."

(2) "Now this, O Bhikkhus, is The Noble Truth of the cause of suffering:– It is the craving which produces rebirth, accompanied by passionate clinging, welcome this and that (life). It is the craving for sensual pleasures Kāmatanhā, craving for becoming Bhavatanhā[7] and craving for annihilation Vibhavatanhā.[8]"

(3) "Now this, O Bhikkhus, is The Noble Truth of the cessation of suffering:– It is the complete separation from, and destruction of, this very craving, its forsaking, renunciation, liberation, and detachment.[9]"

(4) "Now this, O Bhikkhus, is the Noble Truth of The path leading to the cessation of suffering:–

It is this Noble Eightfold Path – namely, Right Understanding, Right Thoughts, Right Speech, Right Action, Right Livelihood, Right Effort, Right Mindfulness, and Right Concentration."

(1) i. "This is the Noble Truth of Suffering–*Dukkha Ariya Sacca.*"
Thus, O Bhikkhus, with respect to things unheard before, there arose in me the eye, the knowledge, the wisdom, the insight, and the light.

ii. "This Noble Truth of Suffering should be Comprehended–*Pariññeyya.*"
Thus, O Bhikkhus, with respect to things unheard before, there arose in me the eye,.......the light.

iii. "This Noble Truth of Suffering has been comprehended–*Pariññāta.*"
Thus, O Bhikkhus, with respect to things unheard before, there arose in me the eye,........the light.

(2) i. "This is The Noble Truth of the cause of suffering–*Dukkha Samudaya Ariya Sacca.*"
Thus, O Bhikkhus, with respect to things unheard before, there arose in me the eye,........the light.

ii. "This Noble Truth of the Cause of Suffering should be eradicated–*Pahātabba.*"
Thus, O Bhikkhus, with respect to things unheard before, there arose in me the eyes,........the light.

iii. "This Noble Truth of the Cause of Suffering has been eradicated–*Pahīnam.*"
Thus, O Bhikkhus, with respect to things unheard before, there arose in me the eye,........the light.

(3) i. "This is The Noble Truth of the cessation of suffering–*Dukkha Nirōdha Ariya Sacca.*"
Thus, O Bhikkhus, with respect to things unheard before, there arose in me the eyes,........the light.

ii. "This Noble Truth of the Cessation of Suffering should be realized–*Sacchikā tabbam.*"
Thus, O Bhikkhus, with respect to things unheard before, there arose in me the eye,........the light.

iii. "This Noble Truth of the Cessation of Sufferinghas been realized–*Sacchikatam.*"
Thus, O Bhikkhus, with respect to things unheard before, there arose in me the eye,........the light.

(4) i. "This is The Noble Truth of the path leading to the cessation of suffering–*Dukkha Nirōdhagāminī Patipadā Ariya Sacca.*"
Thus, O Bhikkhus, with respect to things unheard before, there arose in me the eye,........the light.

ii. "This Noble Truth of the Path Leading to the Cessation of Suffering should be developed–*Bhāvetabbam.*"

Thus, O, Bhikkhus, with respect to things unheard before, there arose in me the eye,........the light.

iii. "This Noble Truth of the Path Leading to the Cessation of Suffering has been developed–*Bhāvitam.*"

Thus, O Bhikkhus, with respect to things unheard before, there arose in me the eye,........the light.

"As long as, O Bhikkhus, the absolute true knowledge regarding these Four Noble Truths under their three aspects and twelve modes[10] was not perfectly clear to me, so long did I not acknowledge, in this world, together with gods, Māras, and Brahmas, amongst the hosts of ascetics and priests, gods and men, that I had gained the Incomparable, Supreme Enlightenment. When, O Bhikkhus, the absolute true knowledge regarding these Four Noble Truths, under their three aspects and twelve modes, became perfectly clear to me, then only did I acknowledge in this world, together with gods, Māras, and Brahmas, amongst the hosts of ascetics and priests, gods, and men, that I had gained the Incomparable, Supreme Enlightenment.

"And there arose in me the knowledge and insight – Unshakable is the deliverance of my mind, this is my last birth, now there is no more rebirth."

This the Blessed One said, and the delighted Bhikkhus applauded the words of the Blessed One. While this doctrine was being expounded, there arose in the Venerable Kondañña[11] the dustless, stainless eye of Truth, 'Whatsoever has arisen, all that must inevitably perish.'

When the Buddha expounded this Dhammacakka, the earth-bound deities exclaimed:–

"This excellent Dhammacakka, which could not be expounded by any ascetics, priest, god, Māra, or Brahma in this world, was expounded by the Blessed One at the Deer Park in Isipatana, near Benares."

Hearing it, the Dēvās of Cātummahārājika, Tāvatimsa, Yāma, Tusita, Nimmānaratī, Paranimmitavasavatti; and the Brahmas of Brahma Pārisajja, Brahma Purōhita, Mahā Brahma, Parittābhā, Appamānabhā, Ābhassarā, Parittāsubhā, Appamānasubhā, Subhakinhā, Vēhapphalā, Avihā, Atappā, Sudassā, Sudassī, and Akanittha also raised the same joyous cry.

Thus at that very moment, at that very instant, this cry extended as far as the Brahma Realm. These ten thousand world systems quaked, tottered and trembled violently.

A radiant light, surpassing the effulgence of the Dēvās, appeared in the world.

Then the Blessed One said:

"Friends, Kondañña has indeed understood. Friends, Kondañña has indeed understood."

Therefore the Venerable Kondañña was name Aññāta Kondañña.

5 THE SENDING OF THE MISSIONERS

The Conversion of Yasa

IN Benares there was a young man named Yasa, son of a millionaire, who led a luxurious life at home. Realizing the vanities of worldly life, he stole away from home at night and went in the direction of Isipatana where the Buddha was staying. The Buddha, seeing him, invited him to His presence and expounded the Dhamma, hearing it, he at first attained Sōtāpatti and later became an Arahant. The sorrowing father, who was looking for his missing son, also came across the Buddha, and hearing the Dhamma from Him, became the first lay disciple (*Upāsakā*) who sought refuge in the Buddha, the Dhamma, and the Sangha. He then invited the Buddha and the Venerable Yasa to his house for alms. When the Buddha visited his house and expounded the Dhamma, the Venerable Yasa's mother and his former wife also sought refuge in the Buddha, the Dhamma, and the Sangha. They were his first two lay women disciples (*Upāsikā*).

The Venerable Yasa had fifty-four friends. Hearing of the Venerable Yasa's conversion, they also entered the Order and attained Arahantship.

Exhortation to the First Missioners

When there were sixty Arahants excluding the Buddha in this world, the Blessed One uttered the following memorable words and despatched them in various directions to propagate the Sublime Dhamma:–

"Free am I, O Bhikkhus, from all bonds, whether divine or human. You, too, O Bhikkhus, are freed from all bonds, whether divine or human."

"Go forth, O Bhikkhus, for the good of the many, for the happiness of the many, out of compassion for the world, for the good, benefit, and happiness of gods and men... Let not two go by one way. Preach, O Bhikkhus, the Dhamma, excellent in the beginning, excellent in the middle, excellent in the end, both in spirit and in the letter. Proclaim the Holy Life, altogether perfect and pure."

"There are beings with a little dust in their eyes, who, not hearing the Dhamma, will fall away. There will be those who understand the Dhamma."

"I, too, O Bhikkhus, will go to Uruvela in Senānigāma, in order to preach the Dhamma."

With this exhortation the Buddha despatched His first sixty disciples in various directions.

Conversion of Thirty Young Men

As it was the rainy season the Buddha spent His first Retreat at Isipatana in Benares. Immediately after He went towards Uruvela. On the way He rested at the foot of a tree.

At that time thirty happy young men went

with their wives to a grove to amuse themselves. As one had no wife he took with him a courtesan. While they were enjoying themselves, this woman absconded with their valuables. The young men, who went in search of her, saw the Buddha and inquired of Him whether He saw a woman passing that way.

"Which do you think, young men, is better – seeking a woman or seeking oneself?" questioned the Buddha.

"Seeking oneself is better, O Lord!" replied the young men.

"Well, then, sit down: I shall preach the doctrine to you," said the Buddha.

They attentively listened to Him and the 'Eye of Truth'[1] arose in them.

Later they all entered the Order and received the Higher Ordination.

Conversion of the three Kassapa Brothers

At Uruvela there lived three matted-hair (Jatila) ascetics known as Uruvela Kassapa, Nadī kassapa and Gayā Kassapa. They were all brothers living separately with Five hundred, Three hundred and Two hundred disciples respectively. With much effort, at times using His psychic powers too, the Buddha at first converted the eldest Kassapa who was greatly infatuated by his own spiritual attainments. Thereupon he with his disciples entered the Order and obtained the Higher Ordination. The other two brothers and their disciples followed suit.

Accompanied by them all, the Buddha repaired to GayāSisa where He preached the *Ādittapariyāya Sutta – 'All in Flames'*, hearing which all attained Arahantship.

The Buddha meets King Bimbisāra

With His large retinue of Arahant disciples, the Buddha, in accordance with the promise He made to King Bimbisāra before His Enlightenment, proceeded to Rajagaha.[2]

The king, hearing of His arrival in his kingdom, went with a large following to pay his respects to the Buddha. As the ascetic Kassapa was held in high esteem by his people, he was at a loss to understand whether the Buddha was a disciple of Kassapa or the latter was a disciple of the former. The Buddha, reading his thought, questioned Kassapa as to why he abandoned fire-worship.

Then the Venerable Kassapa acknowledged the Buddha's superiority, saying:–

"My teacher, Lord, is the Lord: I am the disciple. My teacher, Lord, is the Lord: I am the disciple."

The devout people were pleased to hear of the conversion.

The Buddha thereupon preached the Mahā Nārada Kassapa Jātaka to show that they were similarly converted in a previous birth.

The 'Eye of Truth' arose in them all. King Bimbisāra attained Sōtāpatti. Thereupon the king invited the Buddha and His followers to his palace for the meal. At the close of the meal on the following day the king offered his Bamboo Grove

(*Vēluvanārāma*) for the use of the Buddha and His disciples.

Conversion of Sāriputta and Moggallāna

Not far from Rājagaha in the village Upatissa, also known as Nālaka, there lived a very intelligent youth, named Sāriputta (Son of Sāri). Since he belonged to the leading family of the village, he was also called Upatissa. He had three sisters – Cāla, Upacāla and Sisūpacāla – and three brothers – Upasēna, Cunda and Rēvata.

Though nurtured in Brahmanism, his broad outlook on life and mature wisdom compelled him to renounce his ancestral religion for the more tolerant and scientific teachings of the Buddha Gōtama. His brothers and sisters followed his noble example. His father, Vanganta, apparently adhered to the Brahmin faith. His mother, on the contrary, was converted to Buddhism by herself at the moment of her death.

Upatissa was brought up in the lap of luxury. He found a very intimate friend in Kōlita, also known as Moggallāna, with whom he was closely associated from an infinite past. One day as both of them were enjoying a hill-top festival called the Giragga Samajja, they realized how vain, how transient, were all sensual pleasures. Instantly they decided to leave the world and seek the Path of Release.

Dismissing their attendants and without even informing their parents, they wandered from place to place in quest of Peace.

The two young seekers went at first to Sanjaya, who had a following of five hundred disciples, and sought ordination under him. Before long they acquired the meagre knowledge which their master could impart to them: but unsatisfied with his teaching they left him, and meeting disappointment everywhere, returned to their own village. Ultimately they agreed between them that whosoever first discovers the Path should teach the other.

It was at this time that Venerable Assaji, one of the first five disciples, went in the direction of Rājagaha.

With body well composed, robes neatly arranged, this venerable figure passed with measured steps from door to door, accepting the morsels of food which the charitable placed in his bowl. The saintly deportment of this dignified person at once arrested the attention of Upatissa, who was wandering in the city of Rājagaha.

"Never before have I seen," thought Upatissa to himself, an ascetic like this. Surely he must be one of those who have attained Arahantship or one who is treading the path leading to Arahantship. What if I were to approach him and ask:–

"For whose sake Sir, have you retired from the world? Who is your teacher? Whose doctrine do you profess?"

Upatissa, however, refrained from questioning him, as he thought he would thereby interfere with his silent begging tour.

The Arahant Assaji, having begged what little

he needed, was seeking a suitable place to take his meal. Upatissa, seeing this, gladly availed himself of the opportunity to offer him his own stool and water from his own pot. Fulfilling thus the preliminary duties of a pupil, he exchanged pleasant greetings with him and reverently inquired:–

"Calm and serene, Reverend Sir, are your organs of sense; clean and clear is the hue of your skin. For whose sake did you retire from the world? Who is your teacher? Whose doctrine do you profess?"

The unassuming Arahant Assaji modestly replied:-

"I am still a novice in the Order, brother; I am not able to expound the Dhamma to you at length."

"I am Upatissa, Reverend Sir. Say much or little according to your ability, and it is left to me to understand it in a hundred or a thousand ways."

"Say little or much," Upatissa continued.

"Tell me just the substance. The substance only do I require. A mere jumble of words is of no avail."

The Venerable Assaji uttered a four-line stanza, skillfully summing up the profound philosophy of the Master, in the scientific truth of the law of cause and effect.

Yē dhammā hetuppabhavā –
tēsam hētum tathāgatō Āha
tēsan ca yo nirōdhō –
ēvam vādi Mahā-Samanō

"Of things that proceed from a cause

Their cause the Tathagata has told,
And also their cessation:
Thus teaches the Great Ascetic."

So well did the Venerable Assaji guide him on his upward path that, immediately on hearing the first two lines, he attained the first stage of Sainthood.

Now, in accordance with the agreement, he returned to his companion Kōlita to inform him of the joyful tidings. Kōlita, who was as enlightened as his friend, also attained to the same state on hearing the whole stanza. Overwhelmed with joy at the successful conclusion of their search after Peace, they went, as in duty bound, to meet their teacher Sanjaya with the object of converting him to their new faith. Frustrated in their attempt, Upatissa and Kōlita, accompanied by 250 of the followers of Sanjaya who readily joined them, repaired to the Vēluvana monastery to see their illustrious Teacher, the Buddha.

In compliance with their request, the Buddha admitted both of them into the Order by the mere utterance of the words:–

"*Ētha Bhikkhave*! Come, O Bhikkhus!"

A fortnight later, the Venerable Sāriputta attained Arahantship on hearing the Buddha expound the Vēdanā Pariggaha Sutta to the wandering ascetic Dighanakha. On the very same day in the evening the Buddha summoned all His disciples to His presence and conferred the exalted positions of the first and second disciples in the

Sangha respectively on the Venerable Sāriputta and Moggallāna, who also had attained Arahantship a week earlier.

6 THE BUDDHA VISITS HIS BIRTHPLACE

King Suddhōdana desires to see the Buddha

ON hearing that the Buddha was preaching the Dhamma in Rājagaha, King Suddhōdana was desirous of seeing Him. Nine courtiers, each with a large following, were sent on nine successive occasions to invite the Buddha to Kapilavatthu. Contrary to the King's expectations all nine attained Arahantship and joined the Order. Since Arahants are indifferent to worldly things they did not convey the King's message to the Buddha.

The disappointed King finally despatched Kāludāyi, who was a playmate of the Buddha. He agreed to go on condition that he would be allowed to enter the Order.

He, too, hearing the Dhamma, attained Arahantship and entered the Order. But unlike the others he conveyed the message to the Buddha and persuaded Him to visit His aged royal father. The Buddha, attended by a large retinue of His disciples, journeyed the whole distance preaching the Dhamma on the way, and arrived in Kapilavatthu in two months.

Arrangements were made for Him to stay in the

Park of Nigrōdha, a Sākyan. The conceited elderly Sākyans, without paying Him due obeisance, put forward the younger ones to salute Him. The Buddha subdued their pride by rising into the air and exhibiting the "Twin Wonder".[1] The King, seeing this wonderful sight, saluted Him immediately, saying that it was his third salutation.[2] Then all the other Sākyans paid Him due respect.

Thereupon the Buddha came down from the sky and sat on the prepared seat. The relatives too sat down to listen to Him.

Then a strange phenomenon occurred. Rain broke out, but it wetted only those who wished to be wet, and not others. When the Sākyans marveled at this phenomenon, the Buddha preached the Vessantara Jātaka to show that a similar incident took place in the presence of his relatives in a previous birth.

THE BUDDHA GOES ON HIS ALMS-ROUND

The King sees the Light

As no one invited Him for the noonday meal on the following day, the Buddha, bowl in hand went from house to house in the streets of Kapilavatthu seeking alms together with His disciples. This was reported to the King, and he with agitated heart hurried to the scene and inquired of the Buddha why He thus disgraces the family.

"This is the custom of our lineage, O King" replied the Buddha to the King's astonishment.

"Surely, Lord, ours is the warrior lineage of

Mahāsammata, and not a single warrior has gone seeking alms."

"This royal lineage is yours, O King; mine is the Buddha lineage."

Standing in the street the Buddha then advised the King thus:–

"Be alert! Be not heedless! Lead a righteous life. The righteous live happily both in this world and in the next."

The King saw the light of Truth and attained the first stage of Sainthood.

Soon he took the bowl from the Buddha and conducted Him and His disciples to the palace and served them all with food. After the meal the Buddha preached the Dhamma thus:–

"Lead a righteous life, and not one that is corrupt. The righteous live happily both in this world and in the next."

Thereupon the King attained *Sakadāgāmi–Once Returner*, the second stage of Sainthood, and Mahā Pajāpati Gōtami attained the first stage of Sainthood.

On a later occasion, hearing the Dhammapala Jātaka, the King attained *Anāgāmi–Never-Returner*, the third stage of Sainthood.

On his death-bed, the King heard the Dhamma from the Buddha for the last time and attained Arahantship.

The Buddha and Princess Yasōdharā

When the Buddha visited the palace, all but Princess Yasōdharā came to pay their reverence to the Buddha. Yasōdharā thought:–

"Certainly if there is any virtue in me, the noble Lord Himself will come to my presence. Then will I reverence Him."

The Buddha handed His bowl to the King, and accompanied by His two chief disciples entered the chamber of Yasōdharā and sat on the prepared seat, saying:–

"Let the King's daughter reverence as she likes. Say nothing."

Swiftly she came, clasped His ankles, and placing her head on His feet, reverenced Him as she liked.

The King then commented on her great love and said:–

"Lord, when my daughter heard that you were wearing yellow robes, she also robed herself in yellow; when she heard that You were taking one meal a day, she also did the same; when she heard that You had given up lofty couches, she lay on a low couch; when she heard that You had given up garlands and scents, she also gave them up; when her relatives sent messages to say that they maintain her, she did not even look at a single one. So virtuous was my daughter!"

"Not only in this birth but in a previous birth, too, she protected me, O King," remarked the Buddha and cited the Candakinnara Jātaka.

Consoling her with these words, the Buddha left the palace.

After the death of King Suddhōdana, when Mahā Pajāpati Gōtami became a Bhikkhuni,

Yasōdharā also entered the Order and later attained Arahantship.

It may be mentioned that Princess Yasōdharā was of the same age as the Buddha.

The Buddha and His stepbrother Nanda

Two days after the arrival of the Buddha in Kapilavatthu, Prince Nanda, the son of Queen Pajāpati Gōtami, was celebrating his consecration ceremony, marriage ceremony, and the house-warming ceremony. It was on the occasion of these three festivals that the Buddha visited the palace. The Buddha handed the bowl to Prince Nanda and uttering a Blessing rose to go without taking the bowl. The Prince followed Him. Princess Janapada Kalyāni seeing Nanda following the Buddha said:–

"Return quickly, O noble Lord!" Prince Nanda was deeply moved by these words that fell from the mouth of his fiancee, but with deference to the Buddha he could not return the bowl to Him. So, bowl in hand, he went to the park with the Buddha and was asked to join the Order. With reluctance he entered the Order out of respect for Him as a Buddha and as an elder brother of his; but he was constantly thinking of his fiancee. The Buddha reading his thoughts devised a means to set him on the right path. With the object of showing him celestial nymphs the Buddha using His psychic powers, took him to a heavenly plane. On the way Nanda Bhikkhu was shown a singed she-monkey clinging to a burnt-up stump in a scorched field. Reaching heaven Nanda Bhikkhu beheld the celestial nymphs and was so much fascinated by them that he compared his charming fiancee to the old she-monkey.

"Would you like to have them, Nanda?" the Buddha questioned him.

"Yes, Lord!" he childishly replied.

"Well, then, I guarantee that you will possess them if you persevere as I bid you."

Hearing that Nanda Thera was living the Holy Life with the object of winning heavenly nymphs, the Bhikkhus ridiculed him, calling him 'hireling'. Eventually he became ashamed of his base motive, and by striving diligently attained Arahantship.

The Buddha and Prince Rāhula

On the seventh day after His arrival in Kapilavatthu Princess Yasōdharā dressed up Rāhula and pointing to the Buddha said:–

"Behold, son, that great ascetic of majestic appearance. He is your father. Go up to Him and ask for your inheritance."

Young Rāhula came to His presence, and asking for his inheritance, as advised by his mother, very affectionately said:–

"O ascetic, even your shadow is pleasing to me."

After the noon meal he followed the Buddha uttering much else that was becoming. Nobody attempted to stop him. Nor did the Buddha prevent him from following Him. On arrival at the park the Buddha summoned the Venerable Sariputta and said:–

"Rāhula asks me for his inheritance.

I shall give him the seven-fold noble wealth which I received at the foot of the Bōdhi-tree, and make him owner of an inheritance transcending this world. Ordain him, Sāriputta."

Rāhula, who was then only seven years of age, was admitted into the Order.

King Suddhōdana was deeply grieved to hear of this unexpected ordination of his beloved grandson. He came to the Buddha and humbly requested Him not to ordain any one without the prior consent of his parents.

The Buddha granted the request.

There are several instructive discourses preached specifically to the Venerable Rāhula. Having come of age, he received the Higher Ordination and attained Arahantship in due time.

The Buddha and Ānanda

Ānanda was a cousin of the Buddha. He entered the Order together with the Sākya Nobles – Anuruddha, Bhaddiya, Bhagu, Kimbila, and Dēvadatta. Hearing a discourse from the Venerable Mantāniputta on the nature of things, he became a Sōtāpanna.

As he possessed a powerful retentive memory, and as he had the rare privilege of listening to all the discourses of the Buddha owing to his close association with Him, he was later appointed the "Treasurer of the Dhamma–*Dhamma-Bhāndāgārika.*"

From the 55th year of the Buddha, until His

Parinibbāna in the 80th year, the Venerable Ānanda ministered to all His needs acting as His favourite attendant.

It was he who pleaded for the establishment of the Order of Nuns. At the First Council he was chosen to rehearse the Dhamma. Thus every Sutta begins with his words – "Evam me sutam. – *Thus have I heard.*"

As he was expected to take a leading part in the First Council which was composed only of Arahants, he strove hard and attained Arahantship on the night preceding the Convocation while he was about to lie down on his couch. It is stated that he was the only disciple who attained Arahantship free from the postures of sitting, standing, walking or sleeping.

The Buddha and Dēvadatta

Dēvadatta was the son of Suppabuddha, and hence the cousin and brother-in-law of the Buddha. He entered the Order in the early part of the Buddha's ministry, and was distinguished for psychic powers (Iddhi). Later, overcome by worldly gain and honour, he so completely changed his life that he became the greatest adversary of the Buddha.

He once approached the Buddha and expressed his desire to lead the Order as the Teacher was old. The Buddha refused. Dēvadatta thereafter committed many an evil act for which he still suffers in Avici.

Knowing perfectly well that the Buddha would not assent, but in order to make it a pretext to disparage the Buddha and thereby win the support of the ignorant folk, he requested the Buddha to enforce the following five rules:–

I. that monks should dwell all their lives in the forest,
II. that they should live on alms begged,
III. that they should wear Pamsukula robes (i.e., robes made from rags collected from the dust heap and cemeteries),
IV. that they should live at the foot of a tree,
V. that they should not eat fish or flesh throughout life. The compassionate, far-seeing Buddha declared that those who wished were free to observe them, but He would not make them compulsory.

Dēvadatta made this refusal a weapon to cause a schism in the Order.

Instigated by Him, Ajātasattu caused the death of his innocent and devout father, King Bimbisāra.

Failing in all efforts to destroy the Buddha, finally Dēvadatta himself made an unsuccessful attempt to kill Him by hurling a rock from above on His head.

Books state that in the remote future he would become a Pacceka Buddha, named Atthissāra, as a result of the Holy Life he led before his wicked career.

7 THE BUDDHA'S MINISTRY

THE Buddha's successful ministry lasted 45 years. From His 35th year, the date of His Enlightenment, till His death in His 80th year, He served humanity both by example and precept, with no personal motive. Throughout the year He wandered from place to place, teaching the Dhamma to the people and liberating them from the bonds of Sansāra. During the Rainy Season (Vassāna-July to November) He lived in retirement, as was customary with all ascetics, owing to the incessant rains.

The First Twenty Years

According to the Buddhavamsa commentary, His first twenty years were spent as follows:–

1st. Year – Benares.

After preaching the Dhammacakka Sutta on the Āsālha full-moon day, He spent the first Vassāna (Retreat) in the Deer Park at Isipatana, near Benares. Here there was no special building for Him to reside.

2nd, 3rd and 4th Years – Rājagaha.

When the Buddha visited King Bimbisāra, he

offered his Bamboo Grove (Vēluvana) to the Buddha and His disciples. This was an ideal solitary place for monks as it was neither too far nor too close to the city. Three rainy seasons were spent in this quiet grove.

5th Year – Vesāli.
During this year whilst He was residing in the Pinnacled-Hall at Mahāvana near Vesāli, He heard of the impending death of King Suddhōdana and repairing to his death-chamber preached the Dhamma to him. Immediately after he attained Arahantship, for seven days he enjoyed the bliss of Emancipation and passed away.

The Order of Nuns

Bhikkhuni Sāsana was founded in the 5th Vassāna year of the Buddha. After the death of King Suddhōdana, Mahā Pajāpati Gōtami, desirous of joining the Order, approached the Buddha who was then residing at Kapilavatthu and begged permission for women to be admitted into the Order. For several reasons the Buddha refused and returned to Vesāli. But Mahā Pajāpati Gōtami, without being discouraged, cut off her hair and wearing yellow garments went on foot to Vesāli, accompanied by many other Sākyan ladies, experiencing many a hardship. Weeping they stood outside the porch of the Pinnacled Hall in Mahāvana where the Buddha was residing. The Venerable Ānanda, moved by the pathetic sight, appealed to the Buddha on their behalf. Again He refused thrice but was finally persuaded by the entreaties of the Venerable Ānanda on condition that Mahā Pajāpati Gōtami would agree to observe the following eight Chief Rules:–

1. A nun, even of a hundred years' standing by Upasampadā, should salute a Bhikkhu and rise before him, though he had received the Higher Ordination that very day.
2. A nun should not spend a Retreat in a place where there is no Bhikkhu.
3. Every forthnight a nun should ask from the Order of monks the time of Upōsatha meeting and when a Bhikkhu would come to admonish them.
4. The Pavārana ceremony after the Retreat should be held by a nun in the presence of the Order of both Bhikkhus and Bhikkunis.
5. Major offences of a nun should be dealt with by the Order of both Bhikkhus and Bhikkhunis.
6. A female novice (*Sikkhamānā*) who remains on probation for two years should receive the Higher Ordination from the Order of both Bhikkhus and Bhikkhunis.
7. A nun should on no account rebuke or abuse a Bhikkhu.
8. Nuns should not give admonition to Bhikkhus, but Bhikkhus should admonish nuns.

Pajāpati Gōtami gladly agreed to abide by these eight Chief Rules. By accepting them she automatically received the Lesser and Higher Ordination. The other Sākyan ladies also received.

their Lesser and Higher Ordination. All of them later attained Arahantship. Yasōdharā and Nandā, the daughters of Pajāpati Gōtami, were also admitted into the Order.

In the Order of Nuns Khemā and Uppalavannā were appointed the two chief Female Disciples, as were Sāriputta and Moggallāna in the Order of Monks.

6th Year – Mankula Hill.
Just as He performed the "Twin Wonder" (*Yamaka Pātihāriya*) to overcome the pride of His relatives at Kapilavatthu, here too He did the same a second time to convert others.

7th Year – Tāvatimsa Heaven.
A few days after the birth of the Bodhisatta his mother Queen Mahā Māyā died and was born as a Deva in the Tāvatimsa Heaven. In this 7th year during the rainy three months, He preached the Abhidhamma1 to the Devās of this Celestial Plane, headed by His mother Deva. Daily He came to earth and gave a summary of His sermon to the Venerable Sāriputta, who in turn expounded the same doctrine in detail to his disciples. What is embodied in the present Abhidhamma Pitaka is supposed to be this detailed exposition of the Dhamma by Him.

It is stated that on hearing these philosophical discourses the mother Deva attained the First Stage of Sainthood.

8th Year – Bhesakāla Forest.
near Sumsumāra Rock, in the Bhagga District.

9th Year – Kōsambi.
It was in this year that Māgandiya harboured a grudge against the Buddha for what He uttered when her father proposed to give her in marriage to Him.

10th Year – Pārileyyaka Forest.
Owing to some unfortunate dispute that could not be settled between two parties of Bhikkhus, the Buddha retired to this forest for the Retreat. It was on this occasion, according to the story, that an elephant and a monkey ministered to His needs.

11th Year – Ekanālā, Brahmin village.
The interesting Kasibhāradvāja Sutta was delivered here.

12th Year – Vēranjā.
During this period the Buddha and His disciples were compelled to live on food used for horses. The stay at Vēranjā forms the introduction to the Vinaya.

13th Year – Cāliya Rock.

14th Year – Jētavana Monastery, Sāvatthi.
The Venerable Rāhula received his Higher Ordination at this time on the completion of his 20th year.

15th Year – Kapilavatthu.
The tragic death of King Suppabuddha, the father of Princess Yasōdhara, occurred in this year. It should be noted that the Buddha spent only one Retreat in his birthplace.

16th Year – City of Ālavaka.
The conversion of Ālavaka, the demon, who feasted on human flesh, took place on this occasion.

17th Year – Rājagaha.

18th Year – Cāliya Rock.

19th and 20th Year – Rājagaha

Angulimāla
It was in the 20th year that the Buddha converted the notorious murderer Angulimāla. Ahimsaka – Innocent – was his original name. He belonged to a distinguished family, and was the most illustrious and favourite pupil of his renowned teacher. Unfortunately his associates grew jealous of him, concocted a false story, and succeeded in poisoning the teacher against him. The enraged teacher, without any investigation, contrived to put an end to his life by ordering him to fetch a thousand fingers as a present. In obedience to the teacher, though with great reluctance, he repaired to the forest and started killing people to collect fingers for the necessary offering. Later he wore a garland of these fingers to ascertain the number – hence the name Angulimāla. When he had collected 999 fingers, so the books state, and was ready to complete the number, the Buddha appeared on the scene. Angulimāla made a vain attempt to kill the Buddha, but was eventually converted to the noble Dhamma and was admitted

into the Order. One day as he went on his alms-round he saw a woman in travail. Moved by compassion he reported this pathetic case to the Buddha who then taught the Angulimāla Paritta which runs as follows:–

"Sister, since I was born in the Ariyan clan,[2] I know not that I consciously destroyed the life of any living being."

"By this truth may you be whole, and may your child be whole!"

He studied this Paritta, and going to the presence of the suffering sister sat on a seat separated from her by a screen, and made this Act of Truth. Instantly she was delivered of the child with great ease. The efficacy of this Paritta persists to this day.

In due course Venerable Angulimāla attained Arahantship.

The remaining twenty-five years were spent in Sāvatthi at the Jetavana Monastery, built by Anāthapindika, the millionaire, and at Pubbārāma, built by Visākhā, the chief benefactress of the Buddha.

Anāthapindika

Anathāpindika, the Feeder of the Helpless, was a millionaire in Sāvatthi. His family name was Sudatta. In the course of a visit to his brother-in-law in Rajagaha, to his indescribable joy, he heard that the Buddha was living in a forest close by. He was so eager to meet the Buddha that he rose up very early and proceeded to the spot, passing through a lonely cemetery. It seems that his faith in the Buddha was so intense that a light emanated from his body. With the aid of this light and the encouragement given to him by an invisible being in the cemetery, he reached Sitavana where the Buddha was walking up and down anticipating his visit. The Buddha summoned him to his presence, addressing him by his family name. He heard the Dhamma from the Buddha and became a Sōtāpanna. Returning to Sāvatthi he bought the park belonging to Prince Jeta, covering, so the story goes, the whole site with gold coins, and erected the famous Jetavana Monastery at great cost. Here the Buddha spent nineteen rainy seasons. This monastery, where the Buddha spent the major part of His life, was the scene of many of His sermons.

Several discourses, which are of particular interest to laymen, were delivered to him. Owing to his unparalleled generosity he was regarded as the chief lay supporter of the Buddha.

It was on his suggestion that the Ānanda Bōdhi Tree, which stands to this day, was planted at the entrance to the monastery.

His wife was Punnalakkhana. He had three good daughters – Mahā Subhadda, Cūla Subhadda, and Sumanā. The elder had attained Sōtāpanna, whilst the youngest was a Sakadāgāmi. His only son Kāla, who was at first irreligious, later attained Sōtāpanna, skillfully guided by his father.

Anāthapindika breathed his last after hearing a profound discourse from the Venerable Sāriputta.

After death he was reborn in the Tusita Heaven. Books state that on the very day he was reborn as a Deva he visited the Buddha at night, and extolling the virtues of the Venerable Sāriputta, expressed his pleasure on seeing the Buddha and His disciples residing in his Monastery.

Visākhā

Visākhā was the devout daughter of Dhananjaya, a millionaire. Her mother was Sumanā, and her beloved grandfather was Mendaka.

The Buddha happened to visit her birthplace when she was only seven years old. Though young in age, she was comparatively advanced in Samsāra. As such when she heard the Dhamma from the Buddha for the first time she became a Sōtāpanna.

Books state that even in her prime she possessed masculine strength. Gifted with all womanly charms talented young Visākha excelled both in worldly wisdom and spiritual insight.

She was given in marriage to a non-Buddhist named Punnavaddhana, the son of a millionaire named Migāra. On the wedding day, in addition to a large dowry and an exquisitely rich ornament (Mahālatā Palandana), ten admonitions were given to her. By her tact and patience she eventually succeeded in converting her husband's house to a happy Buddhist home. Her callous father-in-law was the first to become a Sōtāpanna and embrace Buddhism.

Thereafter she was left free to engage in her religious activities as she liked.

It was she who constructed the Pubbārāma in the east of Sāvatthi, as suggested by the Buddha. Here the Buddha spent six rainy seasons.

She became the most prominent lay female supporter of the Buddha and His disciples.

As a lady she played a very important part in many activities connected with the Sāsana. At times she was even deputed by the Buddha to settle disputes that arose amongst the Bhikkhunis. Some rules were laid down for Bhikkhus at her suggestion.

By her dignified conduct, refined manners, courteous speech, obedience and reverence to elders, compassion to her less fortunate ones, and kind hospitality, she won the hearts of all who knew her.

8 THE BUDDHA'S DAILY ROUTINE

THE Buddha performed His duties systematically in accordance with a pre-arranged plan. The whole day He was fully occupied with His religious work, except when He was attending to His essential physical needs. Though, on several occasions, He delivered discourses that tend to worldly happiness, His main concern was the moral upliftment of the people. Himself enlightened, He endeavoured His best to enlighten others.

His day was divided into five parts – namely,

I. the Forenoon Session,
II. the Afternoon Session,
III. the First Watch,
IV. the Middle Watch and
V. the Last Watch.

The Forenoon Session

Usually early in the morning He surveys the world with His Divine Eye to see whom He could help. If any person needs his assistance, uninvited He goes – on foot, as a rule, otherwise according to circumstances, exercising His psychic powers –

and leads him or her on the right path. He went in search of the vicious and the impure; the virtuous and the pure came in search of Him.

Rendering any such spiritual service to whomsoever it is necessary, He proceeds on his almsround, if He is not invited to any particular place, either alone or with the Bhikkhus. Before midday He finishes His meal.

Immediately after the meal He delivers a short discourse to the people, establishes them in the Three Refuges and the Five Precepts, and if the persons are spiritually matured, they are shown the Path to Sainthood. At times He grants ordination if there are candidates for the Order. He then retires to the monastery.

The Afternoon Session

After the noon meal He takes a seat in the monastery when Bhikkhus assemble to listen to His exposition of the Dhamma. Some get objects of meditation according to their temperaments and retire to congenial places. Others pay their due respects to Him and retire to their chambers to spend the afternoon.

Having exhorted the disciples thus, He himself retires to His private 'Perfumed Chamber' to rest. If He so desires, He lies to His right side and sleeps for a while with mindfulness. On rising He attains to the Ecstasy of Great Compassion – *Mahā Karunā Samāpatti* and surveys with His Divine Eye the world, especially the Bhikkhus who retired to solitude for meditation, and others in order to give them any spiritual advice that is needed. If the erring ones that need advice happen to be at a distance, there He goes by His psychic powers, advises them and then retires to His chamber.

Towards evening the lay followers flock to Him to hear the Dhamma. Perceiving their innate tendencies and their temperaments with the Buddha-Eye, He preaches to them for about one hour.[1] Each member of the audience, though differently constituted, thinks that the Buddha's sermon is directed particularly to him. Such was the Buddha's method of exposition of the Dhamma. As a rule the Buddha converts others chiefly by expounding the Dhamma, for He appeals more to the intellect than to emotion. The Buddha advises the seekers of Truth not to accept anything merely on the authority of another, but to exercise their own reasoning and judge for themselves whether anything is right or wrong.

On one occasion the Kālāmas of Kessaputta approached the Buddha, and said that many ascetics and Brahmins who came to preach to them used to exalt their own doctrines and denounce the doctrines of others, and that they were at a loss to understand who of those worthies were speaking the truth and who were not.

"Yes, O Kālāmas, it is right for you to doubt, it is right for you to waver. In a doubtful matter wavering has arisen."

Thus remarked the Buddha and gave them the following advice, which applies with equal force to the modern rationalists as it did to those sceptic Brahmins of yore.

"Come, O Kālāmas! Do not accept anything on (mere) hearsay. Do not accept anything on mere tradition. Do not accept anything on account of rumours. Do not accept anything just because it accords with your scriptures. Do not accept anything by mere supposition. Do not accept anything by merely considering the reasons. Do not accept anything merely because it agrees with your preconceived notions. Do not accept anything merely because it seems acceptable. Do not accept anything thinking that the ascetic is respected by us."

"But, Kālāmas, when you know for yourselves – These things are immoral; these things are blameworthy; these things are censured by the wise; these things when performed and undertaken, conduce to ruin and sorrow – then indeed do you reject them."

"When, Kālāmas, you know for yourselves – These things are moral; these things are blameless; these things are praised by the wise; these things when performed and undertaken, conduce to well-being and happiness – then do you live acting accordingly."

These words of the Buddha, uttered some 2500 years ago, still retain their original force and freshness.

On rare occasions, as in the case of Angulimāla, Khēmā and others, the Buddha resorts to His psychic powers.

The sublime Teachings of the Buddha appealed to all alike. There was milk for the babe and meat for the strong in His rational teachings. Both rich and poor, high and low renounced their former faiths and embraced the new Message of Peace. The infant Sāsana which began with five ascetics soon developed into millions and peacefully spread throughout central India.

The First Watch

This period of the night extends from 6 to 10, and is exclusively reserved for Bhikkhus. It is during this period that Bhikkhus get their doubts cleared, question the Buddha on the intricacies of the Dhamma, obtain suitable objects of meditation, and hear the Dhamma from the Buddha.

The Middle Watch

During this period which extends from 10 p.m. to 2 a.m., Celestial Beings such as Devas and Brahmas, who are invisible to ordinary human beings, approach the Buddha to question Him on the Dhamma. Several such discourses and answers given to their queries appear mostly in the Saṁyutta Nikāya.

The Last Watch

The small hours of the morning extending from 2 to 6, which comprise the last watch, are divided into four parts.

The first part is devoted to pacing up and down (Cankamana). This serves as a mild physical exercise to him. During the second part (3 to 4), mindfully He sleeps lying to the right side. Throughout the third part (4 to 5) He attains the Fruit of Arahantship and enjoys Nibbānic Bliss.

The last hour (5 to 6) He spends in attaining to the Ecstasy of Great Compassion – *Mahā Karunā Samāpatti.* At this early hour He radiates thoughts of Loving-Kindness towards all beings and surveys the world with His Buddha-Eye to see whether He could be of service to any. If there be any worthy case, He goes of His own accord and gives the necessary spiritual assistance.

* * * * *

The whole day He is occupied with His religious activities. He sleeps only for one hour a day at night. For two solid hours in the noon and at dawn He pervades the whole world with thoughts of Mettā – Loving-Kindness. He seeks His own food without inconveniencing any. Leading a life of voluntary poverty, begging His food from door to door, wandering from place to place for eight months throughout the year. He tirelessly worked in the foregoing manner till His eightieth year.

9 THE BUDDHA'S GREATNESS

THE Buddha was a unique Being. He was the profoundest of thinkers, the most persuasive of speakers, the most energetic of workers, the most successful of reformers, the most compassionate and tolerant of teachers, the most efficient of administrators, and above all – the Holiest of Holies.

During the early period of His renunciation He sought the advice of distinguished religious teachers, but He could not obtain what He sought from outside sources. Circumstances compelled Him to think for Himself and seek within. He sought, He thought, He reflected; ultimately He found His goal of life. Having discovered the Truth,He opened the gates of Immortality to all who wish to hear Him and seek their Deliverance from this ever-recurring cycle of births and deaths, and not because He was an infant prodigy in the ordinary accepted sense.

As He knew everything that ought to be known and as He obtained the key to all knowledge. He is called *Sabbaññu*-Omniscient. This knowledge He acquired by His own efforts as the result of a countless series of births.

What He taught was merely an infinitesimal part of what He knew. He taught only what was necessary for our Deliverance.

On one occasion while the Buddha was residing in a forest He took a handful of leaves and said:–

"O Bhikkhus, what I have taught you is comparable to the leaves in my hand, what I have not taught you is comparable to the number of leaves in the forest."

Daily He preached His Doctrine to both the Sangha (ordained disciples) and the laity. In the forenoon He goes in search of individuals who need His advice. Immediately after His noon meal He exhorts and instructs His ordained disciples. In the evening for about an hour He preaches to the layfolk who flock to hear Him. During the first watch of the night He again preaches to His ordained disciples. Throughout the middle watch He receives the Devas and other invisible beings and explains the doctrine to them.

Practising what He preached, He worked incessantly for forty-five long years for the good and happiness of all to His last moment.

The Buddha and the Caste System

Very wisely and very effectively He laboured to eradicate the social evils that prevailed in His day. He vehemently protested against the caste system that blocked the progress of mankind.
In His opinion:–

"Birth makes no Brahman,
nor non-Brahman makes;
Tis life doing that mould the Brahman true.
Their lives mould farmers,
tradesmen, merchants, serfs;
Their lives mould robbers, soldiers,
chaplains, kings.
By birth is not one an outcast,
By birth is not one a Brahman,
By deeds is one an outcast,
By deeds is one a Brahman."

According to the Buddha, caste or colour does not preclude one from becoming a Buddhist or entering the Order. Fishermen, scavengers, courtesans, together with warriors and Brahmins, were freely admitted into the Order and enjoyed equal privileges and were equally given positions of rank.

Upāli,[1] the barber, for instance, was made, in preference to all others, the chief in matters pertaining to the Vinaya. The timid Sunīta, the scavenger, was admitted by the Buddha Himself into the Order. The courtesan Ambapāli entered the Order and attained Arahantship. Sāti, the monk who maintained a deadly heresy, was the son of a fisherman. Subhā was the daughter of a smith, Punnā was a slave girl. Cāpā was the daughter of a deer-stalker. Such instances could be multiplied to show that the portals of Buddhism were wide open to all without any distinction.

It was also the Buddha who attempted to

abolish slavery for the first time in the known history of the world.

The Buddha and Women

The Buddha raised the status of women and brought them to a realization of their importance to society. He did not humiliate women, but only regarded them as weak by nature. He saw the innate good of both men and women and assigned to them their due place in His Teaching. Sex is no obstacle to attaining Sainthood.

Sometimes the Pāli term used to denote women is "*Mātugāma*", which means 'motherfolk', or 'society of mothers'. As a mother, woman holds an honourable place in Buddhism. The wife is regarded as 'the best friend' (*paramasakhā*) of the husband.

Although at first the Buddha refused to admit women into the Order, yet later He was persuaded by the entreaties of the Venerable Ānanda and founded the Order of Bhikkhunis (Nuns).

Just as the Arahants Sāriputta and Moggallāna were made the two chief disciples in the Order of Monks, even so the Arahants Khēmā and Uppalavannā were made the two chief female disciples in the Order of Nuns. Many other female disciples too were named by the Buddha Himself as amongst His most distinguished and devout followers.

Women were placed under unfavourable circumstances before the advent of the Buddha, and this new Order was certainly a great Blessing.

In this Order queens, princesses, daughters of noble families, widows, bereaved mothers, helpless women, courtesans – all despite their caste or rank – met on a common platform, enjoyed perfect consolation and peace, and breathed that free atmosphere which is denied to those confined in cottages and palatial mansions. Many who otherwise would have fallen into oblivion distinguished themselves in various ways and gained their emancipation by seeking refuge in the Order.

His Tolerance towards Dumb Animals

The tolerance of the Buddha was extended not only to men and women but to dumb animals as well. For it was the Buddha who banned the sacrifice of poor beasts and admonished His followers to extend their Loving-Kindness (Maitri) to all living beings. No man has the right or power to destroy the life of another living animal even for the sake of one's stomach as life is precious to all.

His Greatness

The efficient way in which He maintained the discipline of His numerous followers, especially His Orders of Bhikkhus and Bhikkhunis, testifies to His unsurpassed administrative ability. He anticipated even the present Parliamentary system. Lord Zetland writes:–

"And it may come as a surprise to many to learn that in assemblies of Buddhists in India, two thousand years and more ago, are to be found the rudiments of our own Parliamentary practice of the present day."

The most notable characteristic of the Buddha was His absolute purity and perfect holiness. He was so pure and so holy that He should be called "The Holiest of Holies." He was the perfect model of all the virtues He preached. His life had not a stain upon it." On no occasion did the Buddha manifest any moral weakness. Everybody that came in contact with Him acknowledged His indisputable greatness and was deeply influenced by His magnetic personality.

His will, wisdom, compassion, service, renunciation, perfect purity, exemplary personal life, the blameless methods that were employed to propagate the Dhamma, and His final success – all these factors have contributed to hail the Buddha as the greatest religious Teacher that ever lived on earth.

Hindus honour Him as an incarnation of Vishnu. Christians have canonized Him as Saint Joshaphat (a corruption of Pāli term Bōdhisatta).[2] Muslims regard Him as a spiritual teacher. Rationalists treat Him as a great free-thinker.

H.G. Wells, the distinguished thinker, assigned to Him the first place amongst the seven great men in the world. The poet Tagore calls Him the Greatest Man ever born.

Fausboll, a Russian admirer, says:–

"The more I know Him, the more I love Him."

A humble follower would say:–

"The more I know Him, the more I love Him; the more I love Him, the more I know Him."

10 THE BUDDHA'S PARINIBBĀNA

THE Buddha reached His eightieth year. His death was drawing near. His two chief disciples – the Venerable Sāriputta and Moggallāna – had predeceased Him. So had Venerable Rāhula and Yasōdharā.

One day He addressed the Venerable Ānanda and said:–

"Ānanda, whosoever has fully developed the *Four Paths of Accomplishment*[1] – *Iddhipāda* could if he so desires, remain in the same birth for a Kappa[2] or for a Kappa and a little more. Now the Tathāgata has thoroughly practiced and developed them, and he could, therefore, should he desire it, live on yet for a kappa or for a Kappa and a little more."

But the Venerable Ānanda could not comprehend the meaning of this statement as his heart was possessed by the Evil One. He did not beseech the Buddha, saying:–

"Vouchsafe, Lord, to remain during the Kappa! Live on through the Kappa, O Happy One, for the good and happiness of the many......"

For the second and third time the Buddha made the same statement. Still the Venerable Ānanda was silent.

Māra[3]

When the Venerable Ānanda left Him, Māra approached the Buddha and invited Him to pass away.

The Buddha replied:–

"O Evil One! Make thyself happy, the death of the Tathāgata shall take place before long. At the end of three months from this time the Tathāgata will pass away."

Immediately after, the Buddha consciously and deliberately rejected the rest of His allotted term of life.

Later the Buddha mentioned this matter to the Venerable Ānanda, who then reminded Him of His previous utterance and besought Him to remain for a Kappa.

"Enough, Ānanda, beseech not the Tathāgata! The time for making such a request is past. If thou shouldst then have so besought the Tathāgata, the Tathāgata might have rejected the appeal even for the second time, but the third time he would have granted it. Thine, therefore, Ānanda, is the fault, thine is the offence." replied the Buddha.

An Exhortation

On another occasion the Buddha summoned all His disciples and addressed them thus:–

"Behold, O disciples, now I speak to you. Transient are all component things. Strive on with diligence. In no long time the Final Release of the Accomplished One will take place. After the lapse of three months from now, the Accomplished One will attain Parinibbāna."

"Ripe is my age; short is my life. Leaving you I shall go. I have made myself my refuge. Be diligent, O disciples, mindful and virtuous. With thoughts collected, guard your minds. He who lives strenuously in this Dispensation will escape the cycle of rebirth and put an end to suffering."

The Venerable Dhammārāma's High Regard for the Buddha

The ordinary disciples were deeply grieved to hear that the Buddha would pass away in three short months. They came in large numbers to pay their last respects to Him. One Bhikkhu named Dhammārāma refrained from joining them. This matter was reported to the Buddha, and He was summoned to His presence. When questioned as to his absence the loyal and dutiful Bhikkhu remarked:–

"Lord, I knew that Your Reverence would pass away three months hence, and I thought the best way of honouring the Teacher was by attaining Arahantship even before the decease of Your Reverence."

"Excellent, excellent! He who loves me should emulate this Bhikkhu. He honours me best who practices my teaching best," said the Buddha in extolling the praiseworthy conduct of that exemplary Bhikkhu.

The Buddha's Last Meal

Cunda the smith, a rich and devout person, heard

that the Buddha had arrived at Pāvā and was staying in his mango grove. He went up to Him and after listening to a very instructive discourse, invited the Buddha and His disciples for the noon meal on the following day.

The Buddha assented by His silence.

Cunda after that night was over, made ready in his house choice food both hard and soft, together with a large quantity of *Sūkaramaddava,*[4] and intimated the time to the Blessed One, saying "It is time, O Lord! Alms are ready."

Then the Blessed One dressed Himself in the forenoon, and taking bowl and robe, went together with the company of disciples to the abode of Cunda and sat on the prepared seat: Seated thus, the Buddha addressed Cunda as follows:–

"O Cunda, serve me with that *Sūkaramaddava* which you have prepared; but serve the company of disciples with other food – both hard and soft."

"So be it, Lord" replied Cunda and did accordingly.

Thereupon the Blessed One said to Cunda:–

"Whatsoever, Cunda, remains of the *Sūkaramaddava*, bury that in a hole in the ground: for, Cunda, I perceive not in this world of gods, Mārās, and Brahmās and amongst other beings, together with ascetics and priests, and gods and men, anyone who could eat this food and well digest it, save the Accomplished One."

"So be it Lord!" responded Cunda, and buried

the remainder of that Sūkaramaddava in a hole in the ground, and approaching the Blessed One, respectfully saluted Him and sat on one side. As he was seated thus, the Blessed One gladdened him with a religious discourse and departed.

Then arose in the Blessed One, who partook of the meal of cunda, a grievous sickness, dysentery, and severe pains, resembling those of death. But the Blessed One, conscious and reflective, bore them up unflinchingly.

Thereupon the Blessed One proceeded to Kusinārā, accompanied by the Venerable Ānanda.

His Last Convert

At that time there lived at Kusinārā a wandering ascetic named Subhadda. He heard the news that the ascetic Gōtama would attain Pari-Nibbāna in the last watch of the night, and he thought of seeing Him. So he went to the Upavattana Sāla Grove of the Mallas and inquired of the Venerable Ānanda whether he could see the Buddha.

"Enough, friend Subhadda, do not worry the Accomplished One. The Blessed One is wearied."

For the second and third time Subhadda made his request, and for the second and third time the Venerable Ānanda replied in the same manner.

The Buddha overheard their conversation, and addressing Ānanda said:–

"Nay, Ānanda, do not prevent Subhadda from entering. Let Subhadda behold the Accomplished One. Whatsoever Subhadda will ask of me, all that will be with the desire for knowledge, and not to annoy me. And whatever I shall say in answer he will readily understand."

Permission being thus granted, Subhadda approached the Buddha, and exchanging friendly greetings with Him spoke to Him as follows:–

"There are these ascetics and priests, O Gōtama, who are leaders of companies and congregations, who are heads of sects, and are well-known, renowned religious teachers, esteemed as good men by the multitude – as for instance Purāna Kassapa, Makkhali Gōsāla, Ajita Kēsakambali, Pakudha Kaccāyana, Sanjaya Belatthiputta, Nigantha Nātaputta. Have they all, as they themselves claim, thoroughly understood or not, or have some of them understood, and some not?"

"Let it be so, Subhadda! Trouble not yourself as to whether all or some have understood or not. I shall teach the doctrine to you. Listen and bear it well in mind. I shall speak.

"So be it Lord!" replied Subhadda.

The Blessed One spoke as follows:–

"In whatever Dispensation there exists not the Noble Eightfold Path, neither is the first Samana, nor the second, nor the third, nor the fourth,[5] to be found therein. In whatever Dispensation there exists the Noble Eightfold Path, there are also to be found the first Samana, the second Samana, the third Samana, and the fourth Samana. In this Dispensation there exists the Noble Eightfold Path. Here indeed, are found the first Samana, the second Samana, the third Samana, and the fourth

Samanas. The other foreign schools are empty of Samanas. If, O Subhadda, the disciples live rightly, the world would not be void of Arahants.

"My age was twenty-nine when I went forth as a seeker after what is good. Now one and fifty years are gone since I was ordained, O Subhadda. Outside the fold there is not a single ascetic who acts even partly in accordance with this realizable doctrine."

Subhadda then praised the Buddha for His lucid exposition of the Noble Dhamma and seeking refuge in the Buddha, the Dhamma and the Sangha, expressed his desire to receive the Lesser and the Higher Ordination.

The Buddha said:-

"Whosoever, Subhadda, being already committed to the other doctrines, desires the Lesser and Higher Ordination in this Dispensation, remains on probation for four months. At the end of four months, the disciples approving, he is ordained and raised to the status of a Bhikkhu. Nevertheless, with discretion I make individual exceptions."

Subhadda agreed to abide by the regulation, but the Buddha requested the Venerable Ānanda to ordain Subhadda.

In the presence of the Blessed One, Subhadda[6] received the Lesser and Higher Ordination and before long attained Arahantship.

He was the last personal convert of the Buddha.

The Last Scene

The Buddha addressed Ānanda and said:–

"It may be Ānanda, that you will say thus:– 'Without the teacher is the sublime teaching. There is no teacher for us.' Nay, Ānanda, you should not think thus. That Doctrine and Discipline taught and promulgated by me, Ānanda, will be your teacher when I am gone."

The Buddha addressed the disciples and said:–

"If, O disciples, there be a doubt or perplexity in any disciple with regard to the Buddha, the Doctrine, the Order, and the Practice, question me (now) and repent not afterwards thinking – We were face to face with the Teacher, yet were not able to question the Buddha in His presence."

When he spoke thus, the disciples were silent.

For the second and third time the Buddha addressed the disciples the same way. And for the second and third time the disciples were silent. Then the Buddha addressed the disciples and said:–

"Perhaps it may be out of respect for the teacher that you do not question me. Let a friend, O disciples, intimate it to another."

Still the disciples were silent.

Thereupon the Venerable Ānanda spoke to the Buddha as follows:–

"Wonderful, Lord! Marvellous Lord! Thus am I pleased with this company of disciples. There is not a single disciple who entertains a doubt or perplexity with regard to the Buddha, the Doctrine, the Order, and the Practice."

"You speak through faith, Ānanda. With regard

to this matter there is knowledge in the Accomplished One, that in this company of disciples there is not a single disciple who entertains a doubt or perplexity with regard to the Buddha, the Doctrine, the Order, and Practice. Of these five hundred disciples, Ānanda, he[7] who is the last, is a Stream-Winner, not subject to fall, but sure of, and destined for, Enlightenment."

Then the Blessed One addressed the disciples and said:-

"Behold, O disciples, I exhort you. Subject to decay are all component things. Strive on with diligence."

These were the last words of the Buddha.

The Buddha's Last Moment

The Buddha's life was drawing to an end. For the last time He rested on the couch placed between two Sāla trees in the Upavattana Sāla Grove. His disciples were surrounding Him in perfect silence. The Buddha attained to the First Ecstasy – *Jhāna*.[8]

Emerging from it He attained, in order, to the Second, Third, and Fourth Ecstasies.[9]

Emerging from the Fourth Ecstasy He attained to the "Realm of Infinity of Space – *Ākāsānancā yatana*.[10]"

Emerging from this He attained to the "Realm of Infinity of Consciousness – *Viññānancāyatana*."

Emerging from this He attained to "The Realm of Nothingness – *Ākincaññāyatana*."

Emerging from this He attained to "The Realm of Neither Perception nor Non-Perception – *N'eva*

Saññā N' Āsaññāyatana[10]."

Emerging from this He attained to "The Cessation of Perceptions and Sensations – *Saññāvēdayita-Nirōdha*[10]."

Instantly the venerable Ānanda, who was anxiously observing the dying state of the Buddha, remarked that the Buddha had passed away. The Venerable Anuruddha, who was distinguished for his Divine Eye, explained that the Buddha had attained to "The Cessation of Perceptions and Sensations."

Then the Buddha emerged from that State and attained in order to the Fourth, Third, Second and First Arūpa Jhānas.

Emerging from these He again attained in order to the Fourth, Third, Second, and First Rūpa Jhānas.

Emerging from these He attained in order to the Second, Third, and Fourth Rūpa Jhānas.

Immediately emerging from this Fourth Ecstasy The Buddha finally passed away.

As a man He was born. As an extraordinary man He lived. As a Buddha He passed away.

11 KAMMA

KAMMA (Sanskrit – Karma) literally means action of deed. In its ultimate sense Kamma means good and bad volition (*Kusala Akusala Cētanā*).

Every voiltional action, except that of a Buddha or of an Arahant, is called Kamma. The Buddha and Arahants do not accumulate fresh Kamma as they have destroyed all their passions.

In other words Kamma is the law of moral causation. It is action and reaction in the ethical realm.

Kamma does not necessarily mean past action only; it may be both present and past actions. It is not fate. Nor is it predestination which is imposed on us by some mysterious unknown power to which we must helplessly submit ourselves. It is one's own doing which reacts on one's own self, and so it is possible for us to divert the course of our Kamma.

Kamma is action and *Vipāka,* fruit, is its reaction. It is the cause and the effect. Like a mango seed is *Kamma, Vipāka,* effect, is like the mango fruits arising from the tree. The leaves and flowers are like the *Vipākānisamsa* – inevitable consequences.

As we sow, we reap either in this life or in a future birth. What we reap today is what we have sown either in the present or in the past.

Kamma is a law in itself. But it does not follow that there should be a lawgiver. Ordinary laws of nature e.g. gravitation, need no law giver. The law of Kamma too demands no lawgiver. It operates in its own field without the intervention of an external, independent ruling agency.

Inherent in Kamma is the potentiality of producing its due effect. The cause produces the effect; the effect explains the cause. The seed produces the fruit; the fruit explains the seed, and both are inter-related. Even so Kamma and its effect are inter-related; 'the effect already blooms in the cause.'

Kusala Kamma

There are ten kinds of Kusala Kamma or meritorious actions.[1]

They are :–

1. Generosity – *Dāna,* which yields wealth.
2. Morality – *Sīla,* which gives birth in noble families and in states of happiness.
3. Meditation – *Bhāvanā,* which gives birth in Realms of Form and Formless Realms, and which tends to gain Higher Knowledge and Emancipation.
4. Reverence – *Apacāyana,* the cause of noble parentage.
5. Service – *Veyyāvacca,* which tends to produce a large retinue.

6. Transference of merit – *Pattidāna,* which serves as a cause to give in abundance in future births.
7. Rejoicing in others' merit – *Pattānu Mōdanā,* which is productive of merit wherever one is born.
8. Hearing the Doctrine – *Dhamma Savana,* which promotes wisdom.
9. Expounding the Doctrines – *Dhamma Dēsanā* , which promotes wisdom.
10. Straightening of one's own views – *Ditthijju Kamma,* which strengthens one's confidence.

These ten are sometimes treated as twelve. Then Praising of Others' Good Actions – *Pasamsā* is added to Rejoicing in Others' Merit; and Taking the Three Refuges – *Sarana* and Mindfulness– *Anussati* are used instead of Straightening of One's Views.

Praising others' good deeds results in getting praise to oneself. The seeking of the Three Refuges results in the destruction of passions. "Mindfulness" promotes diverse forms of happiness.

The Five Rūpa Jhānas and the Four Arūpa Jhānas are also regarded as Kusala Kamma pertaining to the Realms of Form and the Formless Realms respectively.

Akusala Kamma

There are ten Akusala Kammas or evil actions which are caused by deed, word, and thought.

Three are caused by deed:– namely, killing–

Pānātipāta, stealing–*Adinnādāna* and unchastity–*Kāmēsu Micchācāra.*

Four are caused by word:– namely, lying–*Musāvāda,* slandering–*Pisunāvāca,* harsh speech–*Pharusāvāca,* and frivolous talk–*Samphappalāpa.*

Three are caused by mind:– namely, covetousness–*Abhijjhā,* ill-will–*Vyāpāda,* and false views–*Micchāditthi.*

Killing means the destruction of any living being.. The Pāli term *Pāna* strictly means the psycho-physical life pertaining to one's particular existence. The speedy destruction of this life force, without allowing it to run its due course, is *Pānātipāta.* Animals are also included in living beings, but not plants.

The following five conditions are necessary to complete this evil of killing:–

i a being,
ii consciousness that it is a being,
iii intention of killing,
iv effort, and
v consequent death.

The evil effects of killing are:– short life, diseasedness, constant grief caused by separation from the loved, and constant fear.

Five conditions are necessary to complete the evil of stealing — namely,

i another's property,
ii consciousness that it is so,
iii intention of stealing,

iv effort, and
v consequent removal.

The evil effects of stealing are:– poverty, wretchedness, unfulfilled desires, and dependent livelihood.

Four conditions are necessary to complete the evil of unchastity — namely,
i the mind to enjoy the forbidden object,
ii the attempt to enjoy,
iii devices to obtain, and
iv possession.

The evil effects of unchastity are — having many enemies, getting undesirables wives, birth as a woman or as an eunuch.

Four conditions are necessary to complete the evil of lying namely,
i an untrue thing,
ii intention to deceive,
iii the corresponding effort,
iv the communication of the matter to others.

The evil effects of lying are:– being tormented by abusive speech, being subject to vilification, incredibility, and a stinking mouth.

Four conditions are necessary to complete the evil of slandering — namely,
i persons that are to be divided,
ii the intention to separate them or the desire to endear oneself to one of them,

iii corresponding effort, and
iv the communication.

The evil effect of slandering is the dissolution of friendship without sufficient cause.

Three conditions are necessary to complete the evil of harsh speech — namely,
i a person to be abused,
ii angry thought, and
iii the abuse.

The evil effects of harsh speech are :– being detested by others though absolutely blameless, and a harsh voice.

Two conditions are necessary to complete the evil of frivolous talk — namely,
i the inclination towards frivolous talk, and
ii its narration.

The evil effects of frivolous talk are:– defective bodily organs and incredible speech.

Covetousness has the characteristic mark of thinking "Ah, would this property were mine!" The two conditions necessary to complete this evil are:–
i another's property and
ii adverting to it, saying:– "Would this be mine!" The evil effect of covetousness is non-fulfilment of one's wishes.

Two conditions are necessary to complete the evil of ill-will namely,

i another being, and
ii the thought of doing harm.

The evil effects of ill-will are:– ugliness, manifold diseases, and a detestable nature.

False view is seeing things wrongly. False beliefs, like the denial of the efficacy of deeds etc., are also included in this evil.

Two conditions are necessary to complete this evil — namely,

i perverted manner in which the object is viewed, and
ii the understanding of it according to that misconception.

The evil effects of false view are:– base attachment, lack of wisdom, dull wit, chronic diseases and blameworthy ideas.[2]

The Cause of Kamma

Not knowing things as they truly are does one accumulate Kamma. No Kamma is accumulated by one who has completely eradicated craving and has understood things as they truly are. Ignorance – *Avijjā* and craving – *Tanhā* are the chief causes of Kamma.

The Doer of Kamma

Who is the doer of Kamma? Who reaps the fruit of Kamma?

Says the Venerable Buddhaghōsa in the *Visuddhi Magga*:–

"No doer is there who does the deed,
Nor is there one who feels the fruit."

In the ultimate sense a Buddhist cannot conceive of any unchanging entity, any being in the form of a Deva, a man, or an animal. These forms are merely the temporary manifestations of the Kammic force. The term "being" is only used for conventional purposes. Strictly speaking what we call "a being" is only composed of mind and matter.

Buddhists believe that there is no actor apart from action, no perceiver apart from perception, no conscious subject behind consciousness.

Volition or will–*cētanā,* is itself the doer of Kamma. Apart from these mental states, there is none to sow and none to reap.

Where is Kamma?

"Where, Venerable Sir, is Kamma?" questions King Milinda of the Venerable Nāgasēna.

"O Mahārāja," replies the Venerable Nāgasēna, "Kamma is not stored somewhere in this fleeting consciousness or in any other part of the body. But dependent on mind and matter, it rests, manifesting itself at the opportune moment, just as mangoes are not said to be stored somewhere in the mango tree, but dependent on the mango tree they lie springing up in due season."

Just as wind or fire is not stored in any particular place, even so Kamma is not stored anywhere within or without the body.

Kamma is an individual force which is transmitted from one existence to another.

Classification of Kamma

There are moral and immoral actions which may produce their due effects in this very life. They are called "Immediately Effective – *Dittha Dhamma Vēdanīya* Kamma." If they do not operate in this life, they become "ineffective – *Ahōsi*".

There are some actions which may produce their effects in a subsequent life. They are termed "Subsequently Effective – *Upapajja Vēdaniya* Kamma". They too become ineffective if they do not operate in the second birth.

Those actions may produce their effects in any life in the course of one's wandering in Samsāra, are known as "Indefinitely Effective – *Aparāpariya Vēdanīya* kamma."

This classification of Kamma is with reference to the time in which effects are worked out.

* * *

There are four classes of Kamma according to Function – *Kicca.*

Every birth is conditioned by past good and bad Kamma that predominates at the moment of death. The Kamma that conditions the future birth is called "Reproductive – *Janaka* Kamma."

Now another Kamma may step forward to assist or maintain the action of this Reproductive Kamma. Just as this Kamma has the tendency to strengthen the Reproductive Kamma, some other action which tends to weaken, interrupt, the fruition of the Reproductive Kamma may step in. Such actions are respectively termed "Supportive–*Upatthambhaka* Kamma" and "Counteractive–*Upapidaka* Kamma".

According to the law of Kamma, the potential energy of the Reproductive Kamma could be nullified by a more powerful opposing Kamma of the past, which, seeking an opportunity, may quite unexpectedly operate, just as a powerful opposing force can check the path of the flying arrow and bring it down to the ground. Such an action is called "Destructive – *Upaghātaka* Kamma", which is more effective than Supportive and Counteractive Kamma in that it not only obstructs but also destroys the whole force.

There are four classes of Kamma according to the priority of effect.

The first is Garuka, which means weighty or serious. This Kamma, which is either good or bad, produces results in this life, or in the next for certain. If good, it is purely mental as in the case of Jhānas – *Ecstasies*. Otherwise it is verbal or bodily.

The five kinds of Weighty Kamma are:–

i Matricide,
ii Parricide,
iii the Murder of an Arahant,
iv the Wounding of a Buddha,
v the Creation of a Schism in the Sangha.

Permanent Scepticism – *Niyata Micchāditthi* is also termed one of the Weighty Kammas.

In the absence of a Weighty Kamma to condition the next birth, a death-proximate Kamma – *Āsanna* might operate. This is the Kamma one does immediately before the dying moment.

Habitual – *Ācinna* Kamma is the next in priority of effect. It is the Kamma that one habitually performs and recollects and for which one has a great liking.

The fourth is the "Cumulative – *Katattā* Kamma", which embraces all that cannot be included in the above three. This is as it were the reserve fund of a particular being.

* * *

The last classification is according to the place in which the Kamma effects transpire, namely:–

i Evil Kamma – *Akusala,* which may ripen in the Sentient Plane – *Kāmalōka.*

ii Good Kamma – *Kusala,* which may ripen in the Sentient Plane.

iii Good Kamma, which may ripen in the Realm of Form – *Rūpālōka.*

iv Good Kamma, which may ripen in the Formless Realms – *Arūpālōka.*

Is Everything due to Kamma?

Although Buddhism attributes the inequality of mankind to Kamma as one of the chief causes amongst a variety, yet it does not assert that everything is due to Kamma.

If everything is due to Kamma, a person would

always be bad if it was his Kamma to be bad. One would not need to consult a physician to be cured of a disease; for if one's Kamma was such, one would be cured.

According to Buddhism there are five orders or processes – *Niyāmas* which operate in the physical and mental realms.

1. ***Utu Niyāma*** – physical inorganic order; e.g., the seasonal phenomena of winds and rains, the unerring order of seasons, characteristic seasonal changes and events, the causes of wind and rains, the nature of heat etc.
2. ***Bija Niyāma*** – physical organic order; order of germs and seeds; e.g., rice produced from rice seed, sugar taste resulting from sugar-cane or honey, the peculiar characteristics of certain fruits, etc. The scientific theory of cells and genes and the physical similarity of twins may be ascribed to this order.
3. ***Kamma Niyāma*** – order of act and result; e.g., desirable and undesirable acts produce corresponding good and bad results. As surely as water seeks its own level, so does Kamma, given opportunity, produce its inevitable result – not in the form of reward or punishment but as an innate sequence. This sequence of deed and effect is as natural and necessary as the way of the sun and the moon.
4. ***Dhamma Niyāma*** – order of the norm; e.g., the natural phenomena occurring at the advent of

a Bodhisatta in his last birth. Gravitation and other similar laws of nature, the reason for being good, and so forth, may be included in this group.

5. ***Citta Niyāma*** – order of mind or psychic law; e.g., processes of consciousness, arising and perishing of consciousness, constituents of consciousness, power of mind, etc. Telepathy, telesthesia, retrocognition, premonition, clairvoyance, clairaudience, thought reading – all psychic phenomena which are inexplicable to modern science are included in this class.

Every mental or physical phenomenon could be explained by these all-embracing five orders or processes which are laws in themselves.

* * *

It is this doctrine of Kamma that gives consolation, hope, self-reliance, and moral courage to a Buddhist.

This belief in Kamma "validates his effort and kindles his enthusiasm" because it teaches individual responsibility.

This law of Kamma explains the problem of suffering, the mystery of so-called fate and predestination of other religions, and above all the inequality of mankind.

12 REBIRTH

KAMMA necessarily leads to rebirth. Past Kamma conditions the present birth, and present Kamma, in combination with past Kamma, the future. The present is the offspring of the past, and becomes, in its turn, the parent of the future.

The present needs no proof. The past is based on memory and reports, and the future on forethought and inferences.

Reasons to believe in a Past Birth

The greatest authority on rebirth is the Buddha. Says He:

"With clairvoyant vision, purified and supernormal, I perceived beings disappearing from one state of existence and re-appearing in another. I beheld the base and the noble, the beautiful and the ugly, the happy and the miserable, passing according to their deeds."

There was no reasons for the Buddha to tell an untruth to deceive His followers.

Following His instructions His disciples also developed this retrocognitive knowledge and were able to read their past lives to a great extent.

The development of this supernormal vision is

not restricted only to the Buddha and His disciples. Any person, whether Buddhist or not, could possess this faculty. Some Indian Rishis, even before the advent of the Buddha, developed such powers as clairaudience, clairvoyance, thought reading, and so forth.

There are also some persons who, according to the laws of association, spontaneously develop the memory of their past birth and remember fragments of their previous lives. A few well-attested cases are reported from Burma, India, Germany, England, etc.

Extraordinary experiences of some modern reliable psychists and strange cases of alternating and multiple personalities tend to throw light upon this belief in rebirth.

This phenomenon of secondary personalities has to be explained either as remnants of past individual experiences or as "being possessed". The former explanation sounds more reasonable, but the latter cannot totally be discarded.

In hypnotic states some can relate experiences of their past lives; while a few others, like Edgar Casey of America, were able not only to read the past lives of others but also to heal diseases.

Sometimes we go through strange experiences which cannot be explained but by rebirth.

How often do we meet persons whom we have never before met and yet inwardly feel that they are quite familiar to us? How often do we visit new places and yet feel impressed that we are perfectly acquainted with their surroundings?

In this world there arise Perfect Ones like the Buddhas, highly developed personalities. Could they evolve suddenly? Could they be the products of a single existence?

How are we to account for colossal characters like Confucius, Pamini, Homer and Plato, men of genius like Kālidāsa, Shakespeare, infant prodigies like Rāmānujan, Pascal, Mozart, Beethoven, Raphael, and others, and little children conversant with different languages and certain subjects which they had never learnt in their present life?[1]

Heredity alone cannot account for them, "else their ancestry would disclose it, their posterity, even greater than themselves, demonstrate it."

Could they arise to such lofty heights if they had not lived such noble lives and gained similar experiences in the past? Is it by mere chance that they are born of those particular parents and placed under those favourable circumstances?

The theory of heredity should be supplemented by the doctrine of Kamma and rebirth for an adequate explanation of these puzzling problems.
Is it reasonable to believe that the present brief span of life is the only existence between two eternities of heaven and hell?

The few years we are privileged to spend here, for the most five score years, must certainly be an inadequate preparation for eternity.
If one believes in the present and in future, it is quite logical to believe in the past.[2]

If there be reasons to believe that we have existed in the past, then surely there are no reasons to disbelieve that we shall continue to exist after our present life has apparently ceased.

It is indeed a strong argument in favour of past and future lives that "in this world virtuous persons are very often unfortunate and vicious persons prosperous."[3]

Some discoveries of modern spirituals also tend to prove the existence of a future birth.

The Cause of this Rebirth Process –

The Wheel of Life

In short, Kamma, which is rooted in Ignorance, is the cause of birth and death. As long as this Kammic force survives there is rebirth.

This process of becoming is fully explained in the *Paticca Samuppāda* – Dependent Arising or Dependent Origination.

It should be understood that *Paticca Samuppāda* is only a discourse on Samsāra[4] or the process of birth and death and not a theory of the evolution of the world from primordial matter. It deals with the cause of rebirth and suffering, but it does not attempt to show the absolute origin of life.

Ignorance – *Avijjā*, of the Four Noble Truths is the first link or cause of the wheel of life. It clouds all right understanding.

Dependent on Ignorance arise volitional activities (*Sankhāra*). Moral and immoral activities, whether good or bad, which are rooted in ignorance, tend to prolong wandering in Samsāra. Nevertheless, good actions are essential to get rid of the ills of this ocean of life.

Dependent on Volitional Activities arises Re-linking Consciousness – *Viññāna.*

This links the past with the present. Simultaneous with the arising of Re-linking Consciousness there come into being Mind and Matter – *Nāma and Rūpa.*

The Six Senses – *Salāyatana,* are the inevitable consequences of Mind and Matter.

Because of the Six Senses Contact – *Phassa,* sets in.

Contact leads to Sensations – *Vēdanā.*

Dependent on Sensations arises Craving – *Tanhā.*

Craving produces Attachment – *Upādāna.*

Attachment conditions Kamma – *Bhāva* which, in its turn, determines future Birth – *Jāti.*

Old Age and Death – *Jarā-Marana* are the inevitable consequences of birth.

If, on account of a cause, an effect comes to be, then if the cause ceases, the effect also must cease.

The complete cessation of Ignorance leads to the cessation of birth and death.

The above process of cause and effect continues ad infinitum. The beginning of this process cannot be determined as it is impossible to say whence this life-flux was encompassed by ignorance. But when this ignorance is turned into knowledge, and the life-flux is transmuted to Nibbāna Dhātu, then the end of the life process or Samsāra comes about.

Modes of Birth and Death

Buddhism assesses death to the following four causes:–

1. The exhaustion of the force of Reproductive Kamma that gives rise to the birth in question – *Kammakkhaya*.
   The Buddhist belief is that, as a rule, the thought, volition, or desire which is extremely strong during lifetime, becomes predominant at the point of death and conditions the subsequent birth. In this last thought-moment is present a special potentiality. When the potential energy of this Reproductive Kamma is exhausted, the corporealised, the life-force, cease even before the approach of old age.

2. The expiration of the life-term – *Āyukkhaya*.
   What are commonly understood to be natural deaths due to old age may be classed under this category.
   There are various planes of existence according to Buddhism, and to each plane is naturally assigned a definite age-limit. Irrespective of the Kammic force that has yet to run, one must, however, succumb to death when the maximum age-limit is reached. It may also be said that if the force is extremely powerful, the Kammic energy rematerializes itself on the same plane or in some higher realm as in the case of the Devās.

3. The simultaneous exhaustion of the Repro-

ductive Kammic energy and the expiration of the life-term – *Ubhayakkhaya.*

4. The action of a stronger Kamma – *Upacēchdaka* that suddenly cuts off the power of the Reproductive Kamma before the expiry of the life-term.

The first three types of deaths are collectively called *Kālamarana* (timely death) and the last one is known as *Akālamarana* (untimely death).

An oil lamp, for instance, may get extinguished owing to any of the following four causes:– the exhaustion of the wick, the exhaustion of oil, simultaneous exhaustion of both wick and oil, and some extraneous cause like a gust of wind.

The death of a person may similarly be caused by the above-mentioned four ways.

The Four Modes of Birth

The four Modes of Births are:–

1. Egg-born creatures – *Andaja,* such as birds, snakes, etc.

2. Womb-born creatures – *Jalābuja.* All human beings, some earth-bound deities, and those animals that take their conception in mother's womb, belong to this class.

3. Moisture-born creatures – *Samsēdaja,* such as certain insects that take moisture as material for their growth.

4. Creatures having spontaneous births –

Ōpapātika. They are generally invisible to the naked eye. Conditioned by past Kamma, they appear suddenly, independent of parents. Brahmās, Devās of heavenly realms, Pētās, and miserable ones who are subject to torments and sufferings in states of woe – *Niraya* are included in this class.

There are 31 Planes of Existence. They are:–

(A) The Four States of Unhappiness – *Duggati*, viz.,

1. *Niraya* – woeful states, which are temporary, but not everlasting.
2. *Tiracchāna Yōni* – the animal Kingdom.
3. *Peta Yōni* – the plane of Petas or ghost-beings.
4. *Asura Yōni* – the plane of Asura demons.

(B) The Seven Happy States – *Sugati*, viz.,

1. *Manussa* – the realm of human beings.
2. 6 Devalōkas – heavenly realms.
3. 16 *Rūpālōkas* – Realms of Form.
4. 4 *Arūpālōkas* – Formless Realms.

How Rebirth takes place

To the dying man is presented a *Kamma, Kamma Nimitta,* or *Gati Nimitta.* By Kamma is here meant some action of his whether good or bad. It may be either a meritorious or a demeritorious Weighty Action – *Garuka Kamma,* such as Jhānas – *Ecstasies,* or parricide, and so forth.

These are so powerful that they totally eclipse

all other actions and appear very vividly before the mental eye. If experience has afforded him nothing weighty, he may take for the object of his dying-thought a Kamma done immediately before death – *Āsanna Kamma.*

In the absence of an *Āsanna Kamma,* a habitual meritorious or demeritorious act (*Ācinna Kamma*) is presented, such as stealing in the case of a robber, or the healing of the sick in the case of a good physician. Failing all these, some casual act, that is, one of the accumulative reserves of the endless past – *Katattā Kamma,* becomes the object of the dying thought.

Kamma Nimitta is any sight, sound, smell, taste, touch, or idea which was obtained at the time of the commission of the Kamma, such as knives in the case of a butcher, patients in the case of a physician, an object of worship in the case of a devotee, etc.

By *Gati Nimitta* is meant some sign of the place where one is destined to be reborn – an event which invariably happens to dying persons. When these indications of the future birth occur, if they are bad, they could be turned into good. This is done by influencing the thoughts of the dying man, so that his good thought may now act as the proximate Kamma and counteract the influence of the Reproductive Kamma which would otherwise affect his subsequent birth.

These symbols of one's destiny may be hellish fires, forests, mountainous regions, a mother's womb, celestial mansions, etc.

Taking for the object of the dying-thought one of the above, a thought process runs its course even if the death be an instantaneous one. It is said that even the fly which is crushed by a hammer on the anvil also experiences such a process of thought before it actually dies.

By death is meant the ceasing of the psycho-physical life of one's individual existence. Death takes place by the passing away of vitality – *Āyu,* heat – *Usmā* and consciousness – *Viññāna.*

In the words of a Western philosopher death is merely "the temporary end of a temporary phenomenon." It is not the complete annihilation of the so-called being, for, although the organic life has ceased, the force which hitherto actuated it is not destroyed.

Just as an electric light is only the outward visible manifestation of invisible electric energy, even so we are only the outward manifestations of invisible Kammic energy. The bulb may break and the light may be extinguished, but the current remains and the light may be reproduced in another bulb.

At the death the consciousness perishes only to give birth to another consciousness in a subsequent birth. This renewed life-flux inherits all past experiences.

This new being is neither absolutely the same as the past one owing to its different composition, nor totally different – being the identical stream of Kammic energy – *Na ca so na ca aññō.*

The birth-process of the butterfly may be cited in illustration of this. It was first an egg, and then it became a caterpillar. Later it developed into a chrysalis, and finally evolved into a butterfly. This process occurs in the course of one lifetime. The butterfly is neither the same as, nor totally different from, the caterpillar. Here too there is a flux of life or a continuity.

The transition of the flux is also instantaneous. There is no room for an intermediate state – *Antarā bhāva*. Buddhists do not believe that the spirit of the deceased person takes lodgment in a certain state until it finds a suitable place for its reincarnation.

Rebirth takes place immediately, and there is no difference in time whether one is born in a heaven or in a state of misery, as an animal or as a human being.

What is it that is reborn?
No-soul (Anatta) – Pancakkhandha

According to Buddhism, apart from mind and matter which constitute this so-called being, there is no immortal soul or an eternal ego which man is either gifted with or has obtained in a mysterious way from a mysterious Being or force.

The Buddhist doctrine of rebirth should be distinguished from the theory of re-incarnation or transmigration, for Buddhism denies the existence of an unchanging or eternal soul.

In the ultimate sense a Buddhist cannot think of an unchanging soul, any being in the form of a Devā, a man, or an animal. These forms are merely the temporary manifestations of the Kammic force.

"Being" is only a concept used for conventional purposes.

If nothing in the form of a spirit or soul passes from this life to the other, what is it that is reborn?

In asking this question one takes for granted that there is something to be reborn.

In the past it was argued – "Cogito, ergo sum – I think, therefore I am." True indeed, but it has to be proved first that there is an I to think.

I say that there is no I to think. In one breath I contradict myself. Yes, it has to be admitted that we cannot avoid using conventional terms.

We say that the sun rises in the east and sets in the west despite what scientists prove to us. We cannot strike a place twice although to all appearance we have done so. Everything has changed so soon. Even space has changed at the second moment.

According to Buddhism the so-called being is composed of mind and matter – *Nāma and Rūpā*–

Rūpa or matter is merely the manifestation of forces and qualities.

In the ancient days the Indian sages too believed in an indivisible atom – *Paramānu.* The Buddha analysed this so-called indivisible *Paramānu* and declared that it is only a manifestation of inter-related forces which He termed Paramatthas or fundamental units of matter.

These Paramatthas are *Pathavi, Āpō, Tējō,* and *Vāyō. Pathavi* means the element of extension, the substratum of matter. *Āpō* is the element of cohesion. Tējō is the element of heat. *Vāyō* is the element of motion.

The four essentials of matter are invariably combined with four derivatives, colour – *Vanna,* odour – *Gandha,* taste – *Rasa* and nutritive essence – *Ōjā.*

The four elements and the derivatives are inseparable and inter-related, but one element may preponderate over the other, for instance, the element of extension predominates in earth; cohesion in water, heat in fire, and motion in air.

Mind, which is the most important part in the machinery of man, is also a compound of fleeting mental states. There are fifty-two such mental states. Vedanā or sensation is one, Saññā or perception is another. The remaining fifty mental states are collectively called Sankhāras or volitional activities. These immaterial states arise in a consciousness – *Viññāna.*

Thus the so-called being is a complex compound of five Aggregate – *Pancakkhandha* – namely, Rūpa or matter, Vedanā or sensations, Saññā or perceptions, Sankhāra or mental states, and Viññāna or consciousness, which are in state of constant flux.

One's individuality is the combination of these five Aggregates. There is no permanent soul that resides in this so-called being.

How is Rebirth possible without a soul to be reborn?

Birth is simply the arising of the Khandhās, the aggregates Rebirth is the arising of the aggregates again and again.

Just as the arising of a physical state is conditioned by a preceding state as its cause, even so the coming-into-being of this psycho-physical life is conditioned by causes anterior to its birth. AS one life-process is possible without a permanent thing passing from one thought-moment to another, a series of life-processes is possible without anything to transmigrate from one life to another.

This body – to use conventional terms — dies transmitting its Kammic force to another without anything transmigrating from this life to the other. The future being there will be conditioned by the present Kamma here. The new being is neither absolutely the same as its predecessor — since the composition is not identical — nor entirely another – being the same stream of Kammic energy. There is, therefore, a continuity of a particular life-flux; just that and nothing more.

13 THE FOUR NOBLE TRUTHS[1]

TRUTH is that which is Sacca. It is an incontrovertible fact. According to Buddhism there are four such Truths – all associated with man.

In the Rōhitassa Sutta the Buddha states:– "In this very one-fathom long body, along with its perceptions and thoughts, I proclaim the world, the origin of the world, the cessation of the world, and the Path leading to the cessation of the world."

This interesting passage refers to the Four Noble Truths which the Buddha Himself discovered. Whether Buddhas arise or not, they exist, and it is a Buddha that reveals them to the ignorant world.

These truths are in Pāli termed *Ariya Saccāni* because they were discovered by the Greatest Ariya, that is, one who is far removed from passions, or because they lead to the Ariyan state of passionlessness.

The first Truth deals with *Dukkha*, which, for need of better English equivalent, is inappropriately rendered by suffering. As a feeling *Dukkha* means that which is difficult to be endured (*Du-difficult, Kha – to endure*). Here Dukkha is used in the sense of contemptible (*Du*) emptiness (*Kha*). The world rests on suffering (*Dukkhē lōkō palitthitō*) – hence it is contemptible. It is devoid of any reality – hence it is empty or void.

Average men are only surface-seers. An Ariyan sees things as they truly are.

To one who sees, there is no real happiness in this sorrowful world which deceives mankind with illusory pleasures. What we call happiness is merely the gratification of some desire. "No sooner is the desired thing gained then it begins to be scorned." Insatiate are all desires.

All are subject to birth – *jāti*, and consequently to decay – *jarā*, disease – *vyādhi*, and death – *marana*. No one is exempt from these four causes of suffering.

Impeded wish is also suffering. We do not wish to come in contact with persons or things we do not like, nor do we wish to be separated from persons or things we like most. But our wishes are not always fulfilled. What we least expect or what we least desire is often thrust on us. At times such unpleasant circumstances become so intolerable and painful that weak ignorant folks are compelled to put an end to their lives.

In brief, this body itself is a cause of suffering. Buddhism rests on this pivot of suffering. But it does not allow that Buddhism is pessimism. It is neither totally pessimistic nor totally optimistic. On the contrary it teaches a truth that lies midway between them. Whilst emphasising the truth of suffering, the Buddha suggests a means to get rid of this suffering and gain the Highest Happiness.

The cause of this suffering is Craving, which is the second Noble Truth.

The *Dhammapada* states:–

"From craving springs grief,
from craving springs fear;
For him who is wholly free from craving,
there is no grief, whence fear?"

Suffering exists as long as there is craving or attachment – *Tanhā*. There are three kinds of craving. The first is the grossest form of craving which is simple attachment to all sensual pleasures – *Kāmatanhā*. The second is attachment to pleasures connected with the view of Eternalism – *Bhavatanhā*, the third is that which is connected with the view of Nihilism – *Vibhavatanhā*.

It is this gross and subtle craving that leads to repeated births in Samsāra and that which makes one cling to all forms of life.

This craving is so powerful a force that one has to summon eight equally powerful forces (the Eightfold Path) to overpower this one single foe.

The grossest forms of craving are first weakened on attaining Sakadāgāmi and are eradicated on attaining Anāgāmi. The subtle forms of craving are eradicated only on attaining Arahantship.

The Third Noble Truth[2] is the complete Cessation of suffering which is Nibbāna, the Bliss Supreme. It is achieved by the total eradication of all forms of craving. The Fourth Noble Truth[3] is the Path leading to the Cessation of suffering, which is the Noble Eightfold Path, the *via media* – the golden mean – of the Buddha.

The first two are mundane – *lokiya,* the second two are supramundane – *lōkuttara.*

The first three deal with the philosophy of the Buddha's Teaching, and the fourth with the practice in accordance with that philosophy.

Buddhism as such is neither an ordinary philosophy nor an ordinary ethical system. It is a moral and philosophical teaching, founded on the bed-rock of facts that can be tested and verified by personal experience.

Strictly speaking, Buddhism cannot be called a religion either, because it is not a system of faith and worship which emphasises the existence of a supernatural God. If by religion is meant a teaching (*Āgama*) which distinguishes between right and wrong, and which furnishes men with a guide to proper conduct, then it is a religion of religions.

14 NIBBĀNA

NIBBĀNA is the summum bonum of Buddhism.

Definition

The Pāli word Nibbāna (Samskrit *Nirvāna*) is composed of "*Ni*" and "*Vāna*". Ni is a particle implying negation. *Vāna* means weaving or craving. It is this craving which acts as a cord to connect one life with another.

"It is called Nibbāna in that it is a 'departure' (ni) from that craving which is called *Vāna*, lusting."

As long as one is bound up by craving, one accumulates fresh Kammic forces which must materialize in one form or other in the eternal cycle of birth and death. When all forms of craving are extirpated, Kammic forces cease to operate, and one attains Nibbāna escaping the cycle of birth and death. The Buddhist conception of Deliverance in this escape from the everecurring cycle of life and death which is not merely an escape from sin and hell.

Nibbāna is also explained as the extinction of the fire of lust – *Lōbha,* hatred – *Dōsa,* and delusion – *Mōha.*

Is Nibbāna Nothingness?

To say that Nibbāna is nothingness simply because one cannot perceive it with the five senses, is as illogical as to say that light does not exist simply because the blind do not see it. In the well-known fable the fish who was acquainted only with water, arguing with the turtle, triumphantly concluded that there existed no land, because he received 'no' to all his queries. The turtle, though acquainted with both sea and land, could not explain to the fish the real nature of land.[1] The fish too could not grasp what land was as it was acquainted only with water. In the same way the Araḥants, who are acquainted with both the mundane and the supramundane cannot define exactly what supramundane is by mundane terms, nor can a worlding understand the supramundane merely by mundane knowledge. It is a supramundane state which is to be realised by one's own intuitive knowledge.

What Nibbāna is not, one can definitely say. What it precisely is, one cannot adequately express in conventional terms. It is for self-realization.

Sōpādisesa and Anupādisesa Nibbāna Dhātu

These are not two kinds of Nibbāna, but one single Nibbāna receiving its name according to the way it is experienced before and after death.

Nibbāna is attainable in this present life. Buddhism does not state that its ultimate goal could be reached only in a life beyond. When Nibbāna is realised in this life with the body remaining, it is called *Sōpādisesa Nibbāna Dhātu.*[2] When an Arahant attains Pari Nibbāna, after the dissolution of the body, without any remainder of physical existence, it is called *Anupādisēsa Nibbāna Dhātu.*

Three Distinct Characteristics of Nibbāna

Contrasting Nibbāna with Samsāra, the Buddha says that the former is eternal – *Dhuva*, desirable – *Subha* and happy – *Sukha*.

According to Buddhism everything cosmic, and hypercosmic is classed under two divisions – namely, things conditioned by causes – *Sankhata* and things not conditioned by any cause – *Asankhata*.

Nibbāna is not conditioned by any cause. Hence there is neither an arising nor a passing away. It is birthless, decayless, deathless. It is neither a cause nor an effect.

All conditioned things – and to this category belongs everything in this universe – are, on the contrary, constantly changing without remaining for two consecutive moments the same.

Everything that has sprung from a cause must inevitably pass away, and as such is undesirable – *Asubha*.

That which is transient and undesirable certainly cannot be happy – *Sukha*. Nibbāna, being non-conditioned, that which has not arisen from a cause, is, in contradistinction to phenomenal existence, eternal, desirable, and happy.

The happiness of Nibbāna should be differentiated from ordinary happiness. Nibbānic bliss arises as the result of calming down passions – *Vūpasama,* unlike the worldly happiness which results from the gratification of some desire – *Vēdayita.*

In conventional terms the Buddha says – *Nibbānam paramam sukham* – Nibbāna is the highest bliss.

It is bliss supreme because it is not a kind of happiness that is experienced by the senses. It is a positive blissful state of relief.

The very fact of the cessation of suffering is ordinarily termed happiness, which too is not an appropriate word to depict its real nature.

Where is Nibbāna?

"Just as fire is not stored up in any particular place but arises when the necessary conditions exist, so Nibbāna is not said to be existing in a particular place, but is attained when the necessary conditions are fulfilled."

In the Rōhitassa Sutta the Buddha says:– "In this very one fathom-long body, along with its perceptions and thoughts, do I proclaim the world, the origin of the world, the cessation of the world, and the path leading to the cessation of the world."

Here world means suffering. The cessation of the world, therefore, means the cessation of suffering, which is Nibbāna.

One's Nibbāna is dependent upon this one-fathom body. It is not something that created itself, nor is it something to be created.

Nibbāna is not a sort of heaven where a transcendental ego resides, but an attainment (*Dhamma*) which is within the reach of all.

What attains Nibbāna?

This question must necessarily be set aside as irrelevant, for Buddhism denies the existence of a permanent entity or an immortal soul.

As right now and here there is neither a permanent ego nor an identical being, it is needless to say that there is no 'I' in Nibbāna.

The *Visuddhi Magga* states-

"Misery only doth exist, none miserable;
Nor doer is there,
nought save the deed is found;
Nibbāna is, but the man who seeks it;
The path exists, but not the traveler on it."

The chief difference between the Buddhist and the Hindu conception of Nibbāna lies in the fact that Buddhists view their goal without an eternal soul and creator, whilst Hindus do.

This is the reason why Buddhism can neither be called Eternalism nor Nihilism. In Nibbāna nothing is eternalized, nor is anything annihilated.

As Sir Edwin Arnold says:-

"If any teach Nirvāna is to cease,
Say unto such they lie.
If any teach Nirvāna is to live,
Say unto such they err."

The Light of Asia

15 THE NOBLE EIGHTFOLD PATH

THE Noble Eightfold Path (Ariya Atthangika Magga), discovered by the Buddha Himself, is the only way to Nibbāna. It avoids the extreme of self-mortification that weakens one's intellect, and the extreme of self-indulgence that retards one's spiritual progress.

It consists of the following eight factors:–

Right Understanding – *Sammā Ditthi*
Right Thoughts – *Sammā Sankappa*
Right Speech – *Sammā Vācā*
Right Action – *Sammā Kammanta*
Right Livelihood – *Sammā Ājiva*
Right Effort – *Sammā Vāyāma*
Right Mindfulness – *Sammā Sati*
Right Concentration – *Sammā Samādhi*

1. Right Understanding is the knowledge of the Four Noble Truths. In other words it is the understanding of oneself as one really is.

   The keynote of Buddhism is this Right Understanding. Buddhism as such is based on knowledge and not on unreasonable belief.
2. Right thoughts are threefold. They are the

Thoughts of Renunciation – *Nekkhamma Sankappa,* which are opposed to lustful desires. Benevolent Thoughts – *Avyāpāda Sankappa,* which are opposed to illwill, and Thoughts of Harmlessness (*Avihimsā Sankappa*) which are opposed to cruelty. These tend to purify the mind.

3. Right speech deals with refraining from falsehood, slandering, harsh words, and frivolous talks.
4. Right Action deals with refraining from killing, stealing, and unchastity.
5. Right livelihood deals with the five kinds of trades which should be avoided by a lay disciple. They are trading in arms, human beings, flesh (that is, breeding animals for slaughter), intoxicating drinks, and poison. Hypocritical conduct is cited as wrong livelihood for monks.
6. Right Effort is fourfold — namely,
   i. the endeavour to discard evil that has already arisen,
   ii the endeavour to prevent the arising of unrisen evil,
   iii the endeavour to develop unrisen good, and
   iv the endeavour to promote that good which has already arisen.
7. Right Mindfulness is also fourfold. It is the mindfulness with regard to body, sensations, mind, and Dhamma (Phenomena).
8. Right Concentration is the one-pointedness of the mind.

The first two are grouped in Wisdom – *Paññā*, the second three in Morality – *Sīla*, and the last three in Concentration – *Samādhi*.

Sīla	...	{ Right Speech { Right Action { Right Livelihood
Samādhi	...	{ Right Effort { Right Mindfulness { Right Concentration
Paññā	...	{ Right Understanding { Right Thoughts

Strictly speaking these factors that comprise the Noble Eightfold Path signify eight mental properties (Cetasikas) collectively found in the four classes of Supramundane Consciousness whose object is Nibbāna.

According to the order of development Sīla, Samādhi, and Paññā are the three stages of the Path.

All these stages are embodied in the following beautiful verse:–

Sabba Pāpassa Akaranam
Kusalassa Upasampadā
Sacitta Pariyodapanam
Etam Buddhāna Sāsanam

To cease from all evil,
To do what is good,
To cleanse one's mind:,

This is the advice of all the Buddhas.

Sīla or Morality is the first stage.

Without killing or causing injury to any living being, the aspirant should be kind and compassionate towards all. Refraining from stealing, he should be upright and honest in all his dealings. Abstaining from sexual misconduct, he should be pure and chaste. Shunning false speech, he should be truthful. Avoiding pernicious drinks that promote heedlessness, he should be sober and diligent.

Every follower of the Buddha is expected to observe these five principles of regulated behaviour daily. As circumstances permit he may advance a step further and observe the eight[1] or even the ten precepts.[2]

Whilst he progresses slowly and steadily with regulated word and deed and sense-restraint, the Kammic force of this striving aspirant compels him to renounce worldly pleasures and adopt the ascetic life. Realizing the vanity of worldly pleasures, he voluntarily forsakes his earthly possessions, and donning the ascetic garb, tries to lead the Holy Life in all its purity. It should be understood that it is not absolutely necessary to retire apart and lead the life of an ascetic to be a Saint. The life of a Bhikkhu expedites and facilitates spiritual progress, but even as a layman one could attain Sainthood. There are several instances of laymen who realized Nibbāna without renouncing the world. Anāthapindika and Visākhā were Sōtāpannas, the Sākya Mahānāma was a Sakadāgāmi, the potter Ghatīkāra was an Anāgāmi and King Suddhōdana died as an Arahant.

In the role of a Bhikkhu the aspirant leads a life of voluntary poverty and practises the four kinds of Higher Sīla — Discipline as prescribed by the Pātimokkha, Sense-Restraint, Purity of Conduct connected with livelihood, and Conduct in connection with the necessaries of life.

Securing a firm footing on the ground of Sīla, he then embarks upon the higher practice of Samādhi, the control and culture of the mind, the second stage of this path. Samādhi is the one-pointedness of the mind.

When he gains this perfect one-pointedness of the mind, it is possible to develop the five Supernormal Powers – *Abhiññā,* namely, Divine Eye – *Dibbacakkhu,* Divine Ear – *Dibbasōta,* Reminiscence of past births – *Pubbēnivāsānussati Ñāna.* Thought Reading – *Paracittavijānana,* and different psychic powers – *Iddhividha.* It must not be understood that these Supernormal powers are essential for Sainthood.

Though the mind is purified, there still lies dormant in him the tendency to give vent to his passions, for by concentration passions are only lulled to sleep. They may rise to the surface at unexpected moments.

Both Discipline and Concentration are essential, but it is Insight – *Vipassanā Pañña* that enables one to see things as they truly are. This is the final stage on the path to Nibbāna.

With his one-pointed mind he looks at the world to get a correct view of life. He now meditates on the Three Characteristics – *Tilakkhana,* Transiency – *Aniccā,* Sorrow – *Dukkha* and Soullessness – *Anatta.* He comprehends that all conditioned things are transient – *Sabbē Sankhārā Aniccā,* all conditioned things are sorrowful – *Sabbē Sankhārā Dukkhā,* and all things conditioned and non-conditioned are soulless – *Sabbē Dhammā Anattā.* Of these three characteristics he takes the one that appeals to him most and intently keeps on developing insight in that particular direction until that glorious day comes to him when he would realize Nibbāna for the first time in his life, having destroyed the first three Fetters – *Samyōjana* – Self-illusion – *Sakkāya Ditthi,* Doubts – *Vicikicchā,* and Indulgence to wrongful rites and ceremonies – *Sīlabbata-parāmāsa.*

At this stage he is called a *Sōtāpanna* – one who has entered the Stream that leads to Nibbāna. As he has not eradicated all Fetters he is reborn seven times at the most.

Summoning up fresh courage as a result of this distant glimpse of Nibbāna, he cultivates deeper Insight and becomes a *Sakadāgāmi* – Once-Returner – by weakening two more Fetters – namely, Sense-desires – *Kāmarāga* and Illwill – *Patigha.* He is called a *Sakadāgāmi* because he is reborn on earth only once in case he does not attain Arahantship.

It is in the third stage of Sainthood – *Anāgāmi* – Never-Returner that he completely discards the above two Fetters. Thereafter he neither returns to this world nor does he seek birth in the celestial realms, since he has no more desire for sensual pleasures. After death he is reborn in the "Pure Abodes" (*Suddhāvāsa*), a congenial place meant exclusively for *Anāgāmins* and *Arahants*.

Now the earnest pilgrim, encouraged by the unprecedented success of his endeavours, makes his final advance and destroying the remaining five Fetters:–
Attachment to Realms of Forms – *Rūparāga*,
Attachment to Formless Realms – *Arūparāga*,
Conceit – *Māna*, Restlessness – Uddhacca, and
Ignorance – *Avijjā* – becomes a Perfect Saint by attaining *Arahantship*.

Thereafter he lives as long as his Reproductive Kammic force lasts. On the dissolution of the body he attains Pari Nibbāna.

16 NĪVARANA OR HINDRANCES

NĪVARANA (*Nī* and var, to hinder, to obstruct) is that which hinders one's progress or that which obstructs the path to Emancipation and the heavenly states. It is also explained as that which "muffles, enwraps, or trammels thought".

There are five kinds of *Nīvaranas* or Hindrances. they are:–

i. Sensual desire – *Kāmacchanda,*
ii. Illwill – *Vyāpāda,*
iii. Sloth and Torpor – *Thīna-Middha,*
iv. Restlessness and Worry – *Uddhaccha-Kukkucca,*
v. Doubts – *Vicikicchā.*

1. Kāmacchanda means sensual desire or attachment to pleasurable sense-objects such as form, sound, odour, taste, and contact. This is regarded as one of the Fetters that bind one to Samsāra.

An average person is bound to get tempted by these alluring objects of sense. Lack of self-control results in the inevitable arising of passions. This Hindrance is inhibited by One-pointedness – *Ēkaggatā,* which is one of the five characteristics of Jhāna. It is attenuated on attaining Sakadāgāmi and completely eradicated on attaining Anāgāmi. Subtle forms of attachment such as Rūpa Rāga and Arūpa Rāga (Attachment to Realms of Form and Formless Realms) are eradicated only on attaining Arahantship.

The six following conditions tend to the eradication of sense-desires:–

i. perceiving the loathsomeness of the object,
ii. constant meditation on loathsomeness,
iii. sense-restraint,
iv. moderation in food,
v. good friendship, and
vi. profitable talk.

2. Vyāpāda is illwill or aversion. A desirable object leads to attachment, whilst an undesirable one leads to aversion. These are the two great fires that burn the whole world. Aided by ignorance, these two produce all the suffering in the world.

Illwill is inhibited by *Pīti* or joy which is one of the Jhāna factors. It is attenuated on attaining Sakadāgāmi, and eradicated on attaining Anāgāmi.

The six following conditions tend to the eradication of illwill:–

i. perceiving the object with thoughts of goodwill,
ii. constant meditation on loving-kindness (Metta),
iii. thinking that Kamma is one's own,
iv. adherence to that view,

v. good friendship, and
vi. profitable talk.

3. Thīna or Sloth is explained as a morbid state of the mind, and Middha as a morbid state of the mental properties. A stolid mind is as "inert as a bat hanging to a tree, or as molasses cleaving to a stick, or as a lump of butter too stiff for spreading." Sloth and torpor should not be understood as bodily drowsiness, because Arahants,who have destroyed these two states, also experience bodily fatigue. These two promote mental inertness and are opposed to strenuous effort – *Viriya*. They are inhibited by the Jhāna factor, *vitakka* or initial application, and are eradicated on attaining Arahantship.

The six following conditions tend to the eradication of Sloth and Torpor:–

i. reflection on
'the object of moderation in food',
ii. changing of bodily postures,
iii. contemplation on
the object of light (*ālōkasaññā*),
iv. living in the open air,
v. good friendship, and
vi. profitable talk.

4. Uddhacca is mental restlessness or excitement of the mind. It is a mental state associated with all types of immoral consciousness. As a rule an evil is done with some excitement or restlessness.

Kukkucca is worry. It is either repentance over the committed evil or over the unfulfilled good. Repentance over one's evil does not exempt one from its inevitable consequences. The best repentance is the will not to repeat that evil.

Both these hindrances are inhibited by the Jhāna factor, Sukka or happiness. Restlessness is eradicated on attaining Arahantship, and worry is eradicated on attaining Anāgāmi.

The six following conditions tend to the eradication of these two states:–

i. erudition or learning,
ii. questioning or discussion,
iii. understanding the nature of the Vinaya discipline,
iv. association with senior monks,
v. good friendship, and
vi. profitable talk.

5. *Vicikicchā* is doubt or perplexity. That which is devoid of the remedy of wisdom is *vicikicchā* (*vi*=devoid; *cikicchā*=wisdom). It is also explained as vexation due to perplexed thinking (*Vici*=seeking; *kicchā*=vexation).

Here *Vicikicchā* is not used in the sense of doubt with regard to the Buddha etc for even non-Buddhists inhibit it and gain Jhānas. As a Fetter vicikiccha is certainly that doubt about the Buddha etc., but as a Hindrance it denotes indecision or unsteadiness in one particular thing that is being done. The Commentary explains *vicikicchā* as the inability to decide anything definitely that it is so.

This state is inhibited by the Jhāna factor – *vicarā,* sustained application – and is eradicated on attaining Sōtāpatti.

The six following conditions tend to its eradication:–

i. knowledge of the Dhamma and Vinaya,
ii. discussion or questioning,
iii. understanding of the nature of the Vinaya Discipline,
iv. excessive confidence,
v. good friendship, and
vi. profitable talk.

17 THE THREE COUNCILS

The First Council

THE Buddha passed away in His 80th year on the full-moon day of Vesak. His death was an irreparable loss. All His followers, with the exception of Anāgāmins and Arahants, were plunged in deep grief and were weeping and lamenting. But an immoral Bhikkhu named Subhadda, who had entered the Order in his old age, was the only one that rejoiced over His death.

"Grieve not brothers," said he. "Weep not. We are now delivered of that Great Ascetic. He constantly worried us, saying 'This is suitable, this is not suitable.' Now we are free to do what we like."

These unexpected words that fell from the lips of a disciple, when hardly a week has passed since the death of the Teacher, induced the Venerable Kassapa, the third chief Disciple of the Buddha, to hold a Council of leading Arahants in order to protect and fortify the Sāsana. The other Theras were consulted, and they all welcomed the suggestions.

King Ajātasattu was informed of the intention of the Sangha, and he made all the necessary arrangements for the Sangha to assemble at the entrance to the Sattapanni Cave in Rājagaha.

Five hundred seats were prepared in the spacious hall, but only Four hundred & Ninety Nine distinguished Arahants were chosen for the Convocation. The vacant seat was meant for the Venerable Ānanda who was then a Sōtāpanna. But in due time, as anticipated, he attained Arahantship and appeared on the scene by his psychic powers to occupy the vacant seat.

The Venerable Kassapa was the presiding Thera. The Venerable Upāli and Ānanda were chosen to rehearse the Vinaya and Dhamma respectively.

The first council was held three months after the Parinibbāna of the Buddha, in the eighth year of King Ajātasattu's reign. It lasted seven months.

Tipitaka

The Vinaya being the life-blood of the Sāsana was rehearsed first. It is composed of five books – namely,

I.	Pārājika Pāli – Major Offences	Vibhanga
II.	Pācittiya Pāli – Minor Offences	
III.	Mahāvagga Pāli – Greater Section	Khandhaka
IV.	Cūlavagga Pāli – Smaller Section	
V.	Parivāra Pāli – Epitome of the Vinaya	

The Dhamma consists of Five Nikāyas – namely,

I. Dīgha Nikāya – Collection of Long Discourses

II. Majjhima Nikāya – Collection of Middle-length Discourse

III. Samyutta Nikāya – Collection of Kindred Sayings
IV. Anguttara Nikāya – Collection of Discourses arranged in accordance with number
V. Khuddaka Nikāya – Smaller Collection

The fifth is subdivided into fifteen books:–

I. Khuddaka Pātha – Shorter Texts
II. Dhammapada – Way of Truth
III. Udāna – Paeans of Joy
IV. Iti Vuttaka – "Thus said" Discourses
V. Sutta Nipāta – Collected Discourses
VI. Vimāna Vatthu – Stories of Celestial Mansions
VII. Peta Vatthu – Stories of Petas
VIII. Theragāthā – Psalms of the Brethren
IX. Therigāthā – Psalms of the Sisters
X. Jātaka – Birth Stories
XI. Niddesa – Expositions
XII. Patisambhidā – Analytical Knowledge
XIII. Apadāna – Lives of Arahants
XIV. Buddhavamsa – The History of the Buddha
XV. Cariyā Pitaka – Modes of Conduct

It should be noted that the introductory words in every sutta – "*Evam mē sutam,* Thus have I heard" – were uttered by the Venerable Ānanda Thera.

The Abhidhamma, according to tradition, was rehearsed by all the Arahants that were present at the Convocation. It consists of the following seven books:–

I. Dhamma Sangani – Classification of Dhammas
II. Vibhanga – The Book of Divisions

III. Kathāvatthu – Points of Controversy[1]
IV. Puggala Paññatti – Description of Individuals
V. Dhātukathā – Discussion with reference to Elements
VI. Yamaka – The Book of the Pairs
VII. Patthāna – The Book of Relations

All these 31 books are collectively termed the *Tipitaka* (Three Baskets). The *First Vinaya Pitaka* (Basket of Discipline) mainly deals with rules and regulations which the Buddha promulgated, as occasion arose for the future discipline of the Order of Monks (Bhikkhus) and Nuns (Bhikkhunis). The Sutta Pitaka (Basket of Discourses) consists chiefly of discourses delivered by the Buddha on various occasions. Some discourses delivered by the Venerable *Sāriputta, Moggallāna,* Ānanda, etc., are also included in it. The *Abhidhamma Pitaka* (Basket of Ultimate Doctrine) contains the profound philosophy of the Buddha's Teaching.

The Tipitaka was first committed to writing at Aluvihara in Sri Lanka about 80 B.C. in the reign of king Vatthagāmanī Abhaya.

The Second Council

The Second Council was held at Vesāli in the tenth year of King Kālāsōka's reign, 100 years after the Parinibbāna of the Buddha.

Ten Unlawful Points

At that time in Vesāli many shameless Bhikkhus of the Vajji clan claimed that the following ten points[2] were not unlawful:-

1. ***Singilōnakappa,*** it is fit to use salt in horns etc. in order to season unsalted foods.
2. ***Dvangulakappa,*** it is fit to eat food as long as the sun's shadow has not passed the meridian by more than two fingers' breadth.
3. ***Gāmaṇtarakappa,*** it is fit for a Bhikkhu who has already finished his meal to eat another meal without going through the due Vinaya rite if he intends to enter a village.
4. ***Āvāsakappa,*** it is fit to perform the Uposatha ceremony in separate buildings in the case of a large Simā (Jurisdiction).
5. ***Anumatikappa,*** it is fit to perform any Vinaya ceremony first and then take the consent of the absent Bhikkhus.
6. ***Ācinnakappa,*** it is fit to conform to the practice of teachers and preceptors.
7. ***Amathitakappa,*** it is fit for a Bhikkhu who has finished his meal to drink that milk which has changed its original state but has not yet become curd, without getting the due Vinaya rite done.
8. ***Jalōgikappa,*** it is fit to drink unfermented palm-wine.
9. ***Adasaka-nisīdanakappa,*** it is fit to use mats without fringes.
10. ***Jātarupadikappa,*** it is fit to accept gold and silver.

The Venerable Yasa, who came to hear of these heretical teachings, resolved even at the cost of his life to nip them in the bud. He succeeded. The Venerable Rēvata who was questioned about them pronounced that they were all unlawful.

Ultimately, in the presence of eight distinguished Arahants who had assembled at Vālukārāma in Vesāli, the Venerable Sabbakāmi, the most senior Arahant, being One hundred and Twenty years from his Upasampadā, questioned by the Venerable Revata, adjudged that they were all unlawful according to the Vinaya.

After which the Venerable Rēvata chose Seven hundred distinguished Arahants to hold a Council in order to protect the Dhamma. This second council lasted eight months. King Kālāsōka acted as the Royal Patron. The Venerable Sabbakāmi was the presiding Thera.

Amongst the assembled Arahants Sabbakāmi, Sālha, Rēvata, Khujjasōbhita, Yasa, Sambhūta and Sānavāsika, all pupils of the Venerable Ānanda, and Vasabhagāmika and Sumana, pupils of the Venerable Anuruddha had the good fortune to live in the Buddha's own time.

The Third Council

The conversion of King Dharmāsōka was a very great asset to Buddhism. With his royal patronage Buddhism flourished, and the Sāsana gradually grew up in importance and numbers. Tempted by worldly gain, many undesirables of alien sects joined the Order and polluted the Sāsana by their corrupt lives and heretical views.

The Venerable Moggalīputta Tissa, who was then the senior Arahant, being aware of the pollution of the Order, refrained from performing the Upōsatha Ceremony with the Sangha for seven years, and was living in retirement on the banks of Ahoganga.

It was at this time King Dharmāsōka entertained a doubt about thoughtless act done by an irresponsible minister. He was told that Arahant Moggalīputta Tissa would be able to clear his doubt. The King sent word to the Arahant, but he would not come. Failing twice, the third time he sent a messenger inviting him to come to protect the Sāsana. The Venerable Thera accepted the invitation and arrived at Pātaliputra. The King received him with due honour and accommodated him in Asōkārāma, built by the King himself. For seven days the King stayed with him, and studied the Dhamma sitting at his feet.

The Bhikkhus were then tested with regard to their views, and the undesirables were eliminated from the Noble Order.

The pure Bhikkhus that remained performed the Upōsatha for the first time after seven years. The Arahant Moggalīputta Tissa availed himself of this opportunity to hold the third Council in order to protect the Dhamma and the Sāsana.

One Thousand Arahants participated in the Council which was held at Asōkārāma, in Pātaliputra (Patna) in the 18th year of King Asōka's reign, about Two hundred and Thirty Six years after the Parinibbana of the Buddha. The Venerable Moggalīputta Tissa was the presiding Thera, and it was he who was responsible for the composition of the Kathāvatthu-Pakarana, one of the seven books of the Abhidhamma, at this august Assembly.

18 ASŌKA AND HIS MISSIONS

THERE reigned in the newly founded city of Patnā (Pātaliputra), a Mauryan king named Candragupta. King Bindusara was his son, and he had sixteen wives who bore him One hundred and One sons. Of them Asōka was the most distinguished. His mother was Subhadrāngi, also known as "Dharma", Sumana or Susima was his eldest stepbrother, Tissa, also called Vitasōka or Vigatasōka, was his younger uterine brother.

Asōka's Family

Asōka had five wives. Whilst he was acting as vice-regent in Avanti, he married a Sākyan princess named Devi. Kāruvaki, Asandhimitrā (Chief Queen), Padmavati and Tisyarashitā were his other wives.

He had four sons and two daughters, Mahinda and Sanghamittā were the children of Devi. Tivasa was the son of Karuvāki, and Kunāla was the son of Padmāvati. He had another son named Jalauka and a daughter named Cārumati.

Aggimukha, the husband of Sanghamittā, and Devapāla Kshatriya of Lalitapura in Nepal, the husband of Çārumati, were his sons-in-law.

Prince Dasaratha, who succeeded him, Sampati, son of Kunāla, and Sumana, son of Sanghamitta, were his grandsons.

Asōka becomes King

In the opinion of some scholars Asōka was born in 304 B.C. According to Pali Chronicles he was anointed King Two hundred and Eighteen years after Parinibbāna of the Buddha, but his accession took place four years later. He reigned Thirty Seven years after his coronation. He probably ascended the throne in his 30th year, and died in his Seventy One year.[1]

The Pāli Chronicles state that Asōka, in his ambition for supreme sovereignty, killed all his brothers except his uterine brother Tissa, who later entered the Order and attained Arahantship. Some scholars do not accept this tradition as some Edicts prove that some of his brothers were still alive after his coronation.

Owing to his murderous attacks on his brothers and the indescribable suffering caused to many a family by his unjust wars, he was stigmatized Candasōka, Asōka the Wicked. But after his conversion to Buddhism he became such an exemplary monarch that his name was changed into Dharmasōka, Asōka the Righteous. Devanampiya – Dear to the Gods, Piyadasi – Pleasant to Behold, were some of his well-merited epithets.

His Conversion to Buddhism

In accordance with the custom of the royal

household, King Asōka regularly bestowed alms on the Brahmin priests. But he was not pleased with their demeanour. One day, whilst he was quite casually looking through the window, he saw a dignified-looking young novice, about twelve years of age, quietly walking along the street with restrained senses. He was invited to the palace and was requested to occupy a suitable seat. Seeing no spiritual superior to him, he ascended the throne. The King thought "Assuredly he will be the head of this place." He then entertained him with due honour, and taking a low seat listened to his exposition of the Dhamma. The young novice Nigrōdha delivered an instructive discourse on the following stanza of the Dhammapada:–

> " Heedfulness is the path to Deathlessness.
> Heedfulness is the path to death.
> The Heedful do not die,
> the Heedful are like unto the dead."

The word of the Buddha appealed to him, and he became a Buddhist. His conversion was the turning-point of his career. Gradually he reformed himself. His outlook on life was completely changed. He modified his way and means. He preferred the Dharma Vijaya — righteous domination — to Dig Vijaya — word domination. Later in life he became such a devout and righteous monarch that H.G. Wells says:– "Amidst the tens of thousand names of monarchs that crowd the columns of history, their majesties and graciousnesses and serenities and royal highnesses and the like, the name of Asōka shines, and shines almost alone a star. From the Volga to Japan his name is still honoured. China, Tibet, and even India, though it has left his doctrine, preserve the tradition of his greatness. More living men cherish his memory today than has ever heard the names of Constantine or Charlemagne."

Although he embraced Buddhism after meeting the novice Nigrōdha, he did not give up his ambition of expanding his empire. It was after the Kālinga war that he became a genuine Buddhist by abandoning all warfare. Wells says he is the only monarch on record who abandoned warfare after victory.

He thereafter became an ideal Buddhist monarch. With ceaseless energy he worked for the dissemination of the Dhamma, not only in India and other parts of Asia but also in Europe and Africa. He transformed Buddhism into a world religion. He made the important teachings of the Buddha popular by his numerous interesting rock edicts. He erected so many *Vihāras* (monasteries) round about Patnā (Pātaliputra) that the whole province came to be known as *Vihāra,* now *Bihār.* He made pilgrimages to almost all the sacred places connected with the life of the Buddha, and lasting monuments were erected to mark those historic spots. Even the slaughtering of animals in the palace for household consumption was gradually lessened and stopped, and he forbade animal sacrifice. As Pandit Nehru says –

"Asōka's example and the spread of Buddhism resulted in vege-tarianism becoming popular."

With his royal patronage Buddhism flourished in his time, but as a real Buddhist monarch he was tolerant towards all faiths. One edict says:–

> "All sects deserve reverence for some reason or other. By thus acting a man exalts his own sect and at the same time does service to the sects of other people."

Asōka was interested not only in the spiritual development of the people but also in their material development. All his subjects he treated as sons. He was so willing and ready to promote the public good that he says:– " At all times and at all places, whether I am dining or in the ladies' apartments, in my bedroom or in my closet, in my carriage or in my palace garden, the official reporters should keep me constantly informed of the people's business. Work I must for the common weal."

True to his words he acted like a father to all. In his time public gardens, medicinal herbs, hospitals for both men and animals, wells, roads, and educational institutions grew up all over the country. To his eternal credit it should be said that it was Asōka who, for the first time in the history of the world, established hospitals for both men and animals, not only in Asia but also in Europe and Africa.

To those hasty critics who decry Buddhism as the cause of the decline and downfall of India,

Asōka's prosperous Buddhist reign is a cogent reply.

Asōka's Missioners

According to the Pali Chronicles, at the end of the Third Council which was held in the seventeenth year of Asōka's coronation, under the presidency of Arahant Moggaliputta Tissa, it was decided to send competent Arahants to nine different places to propagate the Teachings of the Buddha.

The names of the missioners and the places are as follows:–

MISSIONERS	PLACE
Majjhantika Thera	Kashmir & Gandhār
Mahādēva Thera	Mahiṁsaka Mandala
Rakkhita Thera	Vanavāsi
Yōnaka Dhammarakkhita Thera	Aparantaka
Mahādhammarakkhita Thera	Mahārattha
Mahārakkhita Thera	Yonakaloka
Majjhima Thera	Himavantapadesa
Sōnaka and Uttara Theras	Suvannabhumi
Mahinda, Itthiya, Uttiya, Sambala, and Bhaddasāla Theras	Tambapannidipa

It is stated that each mission consisted of five Theras so that it would be possible to perform the Upasampadā ceremony in remote districts.

1. Kashmir is situated in the north-west of India. Peshavār and Rāvalpindi in north Punjab embrace Gandhāra.
   Majjhantika Thera arrived here and subjugated

the Nāga king Aravala by his psychic powers and preached the Āsivisopama Sutta.

2. Mahimsaka Mandala is identified with modern Mysore in South India. According to some it is a country south of the Vindhya Mountains. The Devadūta Sutta was preached here.
3. Vanavāsi is North Kanāra situated in South India. Even today there is a city called Vanavāsi in this country.
   The Anamatagga Sutta was the subject of the sermon.
4. Aparanta (Western End) is supposed to be Western India. According to the Purānas one of the five countries that existed in ancient India was Aparanta. Its capital was port Supparaka, modern Sopāra. North Gujerat, Katiyavar, Kach, Sindh are included in Aparanta. The discourse that was delivered here was the Aggikkandhōpama Sutta.
5. Mahārattha is modern Mahārāshtra, which embraces mid-West India. The Mahā Nārada-Kassapa Jātaka was delivered here.
6. Yōnakarattha is the kingdom of the Greeks. It must be the Greek kingdom that existed in West India. According to some it comprises Egypt, Syria and Greece.
   The Kalakarama Sutta was delivered here.
7. It is stated that the Arahants Kassapagotta, Ālakadeva, Mahādeva and Dundubhissara accompanied the Arahant Majjhima to the Himālaya region[2] and preached the Dhammacakkappavattana Sutta.

8. Some identify Suvannabhumi with Burma. Some say it is Karna Suvarna situated in Bengal, and some say it is Hiranyavaha district along the banks of the Sona river.
   The Brahmajāla Sutta was the subject of the discourse.
9. Tambapannidipa is Sri Lanka (Ceylon).

The Mission to Ceylon

King Asōka's son himself accompanied by four Bhikkhus, one Sāmanera, and a lay Upāsaka arrived in Lanka to convert the Sinhalas. It was on a festival day that they reached Ceylon. They met the reigning king Devānampiyatissa, who had gone with a party to hunt deer on a hill called Missaka (modern Mihintale). The Arahant Mahinda arrested the attention of the king by addressing him simply as "Tissa". An interesting conversation then followed. After this the Arahant Mahinda preached the Cullahatthi-padōpama Sutta to the king and his followers, hearing which they all sought refuge in the Buddha, the Dhamma, and the Sangha, and embraced this new teaching.

The Venerable Mahinda's Ceylon mission was a great success. he found in Lanka a fertile soil to disseminate the sublime Teachings of the Buddha. With royal patronage Buddhism was firmly established in Ceylon.

As Princess Anulā, who attained the first stage of sainthood on hearing the first discourse delivered in the capital of Anurādhapura, expressed her desire to join the Order, the Venerable Mahinda despatched a messenger to India inviting his sister Sanghamittā Theri to visit Lanka in order to establish the Bhikkhuni Sāsana. As invited, she arrived in Ceylon with a branch of the Maha-Bodhi Tree at Buddha Gayā, and accompanied by a large retinue of distinguished men, who contributed largely to the material, intellectual, and spiritual development of Sri Lanka.

To the eternal credit of Sinhala Buddhists it should be said that it is they who protected the sublime Teachings of the Dhamma in their pristine purity by committing them to writing on ola leaves for the first time in the history of the Buddhist world.

19 THE MANGALA SUTTA[1]

BLESSINGS

Thus have I Heard:–

On one occasion the Blessed One was dwelling at the monastery of Anāthapindika,[2] in Jēta's Grove, near Sāvatthi.[3] Now when the night was far spent, a certain deity, whose surpassing splendour illuminated the entire Jēta Grove, came to the presence of the Blessed One and, drawing near, respectfully saluted Him and stood on one side. Standing thus, he addressed the Blessed One in verse[4]:–

1. "Many deities and men yearning after good, have pondered on Blessings,[5] Pray, tell me the Highest Blessing."

The Blessed One answered him thus:–

2. "Not to associate with fools, to associate with the wise, and to honour those who are worthy of honour — this is the Highest Blessing."
3. "To reside in a suitable locality,[6] to have done meritorious actions in the past, and to set oneself in the right course[7] – this is the Highest Blessing."

4. "Much learning,[8] perfect handicraft,[9] a highly trained discipline,[10] and pleasant speech — this is the Highest Blessing"
5. "The support of father and mother, the cherishing of wife and children, and peaceful occupations — this is the Highest Blessing."
6. "Liberality, righteous conduct, the helping of relatives, and blameless actions — this the the Highest Blessing."
7. "To cease and abstain from evil, forbearance with respect to intoxicants,[11] and steadfastness in virtue — this is the Highest Blessing."
8. "Reverence,[12] humility, contentment, gratitude, and opportune hearing of the Dhamma[13] — this is the Highest Blessing."
9. "Patience, obedience, sight of the Samanas[14] and religious discussions in due season — this is the Highest Blessing."
10. "Self-control, the holy life perception of the Noble Truths, and the realisation of Nibbāna — this is the Highest Blessing."
11. "He whose mind does not flutter by contact with worldly contingencies.[15] Sorrowless, Stainless, and Secure[16] — this is the Highest Blessing."
12. "To them, fulfilling matters such as these, everywhere invincible, in every way moving happily — these[17] are the Highest Blessing."[18]

20 THE PARĀBHAVA SUTTA[1]

DOWNFALL

Thus have I heard:–

On one occasion the Blessed One was dwelling at the monastery of Anāthapindika in the Jēta Grove near Sāvatthi.

Now when the night was far spent, a certain deity[2] whose splendour illuminated the whole jēta Grove, came to the presence of the Blessed One, and drawing near, respectfully saluted Him and stood on one side. Standing thus, he addressed the Blessed One in verse:

1. "Having come to interrogate the Blessed One, we ask Thee, O Gōtama, about the falling man. Pray, tell us the cause of one's downfall."
2. "Easily known is the progressive one, easily known is the declining one. A lover of the Dhamma is the progressive one, a hater of the Dhamma is the declining one."
3. "This then we learn is the first cause of one's downfall. Pray, O Blessed One, tell us the second cause of one's downfall."
4. "The vicious are dear to him. In the virtuous he

finds nothing pleasing. He favours the creeds of the vicious – this is the cause of one's downfall."

5. "This then we learn is the second cause of one's downfall. Pray, O Blessed One, tell us the third cause of one's downfall."
6. "The man who is drowsy, fond of society, not industrious, indolent, and who manifests anger – this is the cause of one's downfall."
7. "This then we learn is the third cause of one's downfall. Pray, O Blessed One, tell us the fourth cause of one's downfall."
8. "Whosoever, being rich, does not support his aged mother and father who have passed their youth – this is the cause of one's downfall."
9. "This then we learn is the fourth cause of one's downfall. Pray, O Blessed One, tell us the fifth cause of one's downfall."
10. "He who, by falsehood, deceives a Brāhmana or an ascetic or any other mendicant – this is the cause of one's downfall."
11. "This then we learn is the fifth cause of one's downfall. Pray, O Blessed One, tell us the sixth cause of one's downfall."
12. "The man who owns much property, who has gold and food, but alone enjoys his delicacies – this is the cause of one's downfall."
13. "This then we learn is the sixth cause of one's downfall. Pray, O Blessed One, tell us the seventh cause of one's downfall."
14. "The man who takes pride in birth or wealth or

clan, and despises his own kinsmen – this is th cause of one's downfall."

15. "This then we learn is the seventh cause of one's downfall. Pray, O Blessed One, tell us the eighth cause of one's downfall."
16. "The man who is a debauch, a drunkard, a gambler, and who squanders whatever he possesses – this is the cause of one's downfall."
17. "This then we learn is the eighth cause of one's downfall. Pray, O Blessed One, tell us the ninth cause of one's downfall."
18. "Not contented with one's own wives, if one is seen amongst courtesans and the wives of others – this is the cause of one's downfall."
19. "This then we learn is the ninth cause of one's downfall. Pray, O Blessed One, tell us the tenth cause of one's downfall."
20. "The man who, past his youth, brings a very young wife and sleeps not for jealousy of her this is the cause of one's downfall."
21. "This then we learn is the tenth cause of one's downfall. Pray, O Blessed One, tell us the eleventh cause of one's downfall."
22. "He who places in authority an intem-perate spendthrift woman, or a man of similar nature – this is the cause of one's downfall."
23. "This then we learn is the eleventh cause of one's downfall. Pray, O Blessed One, tell us the twelfth cause of one's downfall."
24. "He who, of warrior birth, with vast ambition, but of slender means, aspires to sovereignty – this is the cause of one's downfall."

25. "Knowing well these causes of downfall in the world, the Noble Sage, endowed with insight, shares a happy realm."

21 THE METTA SUTTA[1]

Loving – Kindness

1. He who is skilled in his good, and who wishes to attain that state of Calm[2], should act thus:–
2. He should be able, upright[3], perfectly upright, obedient, gentle and humble.
   Contented, easily supportable, with few duties, of light livelihood, with senses controlled, discreet, not impudent, not be greedily attached to families.
3. He should not commit any slight wrong on account of which other wise men might censure him.
   May all beings be happy and secure, may their hearts be wholesome!
4. Whatever living beings there be — feeble or strong, long, stout or medium, short, small or large, seen or unseen,those dwelling far or near, those who are born and those who are to be born – may all beings, without exception, be happy-minded!
5. Let none deceive another nor despise any person whatever in any place. In anger or ill-will let him not wish any harm to another.

6. Just as a mother would protect her only child at the risk of her own life, even so, let him cultivate a boundless heart towards all beings.
7. Let his thoughts of boundless love pervade the whole world — above, below and across without any obstruction, without any hatred, without any enmity.
8. Whether he stands, walks, sits or lies down, as long as he is awake, he should develop this mindfulness. This, they say, is the Highest Conduct here.[4]
9. Not falling into Error,[5] virtuous, and endowed with Insight,[6] he discards attachment to sense-desires. Of a truth, he does not come again for conception in a womb.[7]

22 THE VYAGGHAPAJJA SUTTA

THUS have I heard:–

On one occasion the Blessed One was dwelling amongst the Kōliyans[1] in their market town named Kakkarapatta. Then Dighajānu,[2] a Kōliyan son, approached the Blessed One, respectfully saluted Him, and sat on one side. Thus seated, he addressed the Blessed One as follows:–

"We, Lord, are laymen who enjoy worldly pleasures. We lead a life encumbered by wife and children. We use sandalwood of Kāsi. We deck ourselves with garlands, perfume, and unguents. we suffer the use of gold and silver. To such as us, Lord, let the Blessed One preach the Doctrine, teach those things that lead to the weal and happiness in this life and to the happiness of the other world."

Causes of Worldly Progress

These four things, Vyagghapajja,[3] conduce to the good and happiness of a clansman in this very life. What four?

"The achievement of persistent effort – *Utthānasampadā*, the achievement of wariness –

Ārakkhasampadā, good friendship – *Kalyānamittatā*, and balanced livelihood – *Samajīvikatā*."

"What is the achievement of persistent effort?"

"Herein, Vyagghapajja, by whatsoever activity a clansman earns his living, whether by the plough, by trading, by watching cattle, by archery, by ministering to kings, or by any other kind of craft – at that he becomes skillful and is not lazy. He is endowed with reasoning as to ways and means thereof. He is able to do and manage (his job).

"This is called the achievement of persistent effort.

"What is the achievement of wariness?

"Herein, Vyagghapajja, whatsoever treasures a clansman is in possession of, obtained by dint of effort, collected by strength of arms, by the sweat of his brow justly acquired by right means-such the husbands by guarding and watching so that kings would not seize them, thieves would not steal, fire would not burn, water would not carry off, nor ill-disposed heirs carry away.

"This is the achievement of wariness.

"What is good friendship?

"Herein, Vyagghapajja, in whatsoever village or market town a clansman dwells, he stands together, converses, engages in discussions with householders of householders' sons, whether young and highly cultured or old and highly cultured, full of faith – *Saddhā*,[4] full of virtue – *Sīla*, full of charity – *Cāga*, full of wisdom – *Paññā*. He acts in accordance with the faith of those full of faith, with the virtue of those full of virtue, with the charity of those full of charity, with the wisdom of those full of wisdom.

"This is called good company.

"What is balanced livelihood?

"Herein, Vyagghapajja, a clansman knowing his income and expenses leads a steady life, being neither too extravagant nor too sordid, thinking that thus his income will stand in excess of his expenses, but his expenses in excess of his income.

"Just as the goldsmith, or an apprentice of his, knows, on holding up a balance, that by so much it has dipped down, by so much it has tilted up; even so a clansman knowing his income and expenses, leads a steady life, being neither too extravagant nor too sordid, thinking that thus his income will stand in excess of his expenses, but not his expenses in excess of his income.

"If, Vyagghapajja, a clansman with little income were to lead a luxurious life, there would be those who say – 'This clansman enjoys his wealth like one who eats wood-apple.[5] If, Vyagghapajja, a clansman with large income were to lead a wretched life, there would be those who say:–

'This clansman will die like a starveling.[6]

"The wealth thus amassed, Vyagghahapajja, has four sources of destruction:–

I. debauchery – *Itthidhuttō,*
II. drunkenness – *Surādhuttō,*
III. indulgence in gambling – *Akkhadhuttō,* and
IV. friendship, companionship and intimacy with evil-doers.

"Just as in the case of a great tank with four

inlets and outlets, if a man should close the inlets and open the outlets and there should be no adequate rainfall, decrease(of water) is to be expected in that tank and not an increase; even so there are four sources for the destruction of amassed wealth — debauchery, drunkenness, indulgence in gambling, and friendship, companionship and intimacy with evil-doers.

"There are four sources for the development of amassed wealth:–

I. abstinence from debauchery,
II. abstinence from drunkenness,
III. non-indulgence in gambling, and
IV. friendship, companionship, and intimacy with the good.

"Just as in the case of a great tank with four inlets and four outlets, if a person were to open the inlets and close the outlets, and there should also be adequate rainfall, and increase of water is certainly to be expected in that tank and not a decrease, even so the four above-mentioned are the sources of development of amassed wealth.

"These four things are conducive to the good and happiness of a noble son in this life itself.

Causes of Spiritual Progress

"These four things are conducive to the good and happiness of a noble son in the other world.

"Which four?

I. Achievement of Faith – *Saddhāsampadā,*

II. Achievement of Virtue – *Sīlasampadā,*
III. Achievement of Charity – *Cāgasampadā,*
IV. Achievement of Wisdom – *Paññāsampadā.*

"What is the achievement of faith?

"Herein a clansman is possessed of faith, believes in the Enlightenment of the Tathāgata:- Thus, indeed , is that Blessed One, An Exalted One, Omniscient, Endowed with wisdom and conduct, Auspicious Knower of worlds, an Incomparable Charioteer for the training of individuals, Teacher of gods and men, Enlightened and Holy.

"This is called the achievement of faith.

"What is the achievement of virtue?

"Herein a clansman abstains from killing, stealing, unchastity, lying, and intoxicants that cause infatuation and heedlessness.

"This is called the achievement of virtue.

"What is the achievement of charity?

"Herein a clansman dwells at home with heart free from the stain of avarice, devoted to charity, open-handed, delighting in generosity, fit to be asked (for alms), rejoicing in sharing alms.

"This is called the achievement of charity.

"What is the achievement of wisdom?

"Herein a clansman is wise, is endowed with wisdom that leads to one's development, and with noble penetrative insight – *Nibbedikāya* that leads to the complete destruction of suffering.

"This is called the achievement of wisdom.

"These four things are conducive to the good and happiness of a clansman in the other world.

"Strenuous in spheres of work, heedful and ordering, he lives well, protecting what he has amassed.

"Endowed with faith and virtue, generous, and free from avarice, he ever clears the path of happiness to the other world.

"Thus for the believing home-seekers, these eight things that lead to the happiness in both worlds – well-being in this and happiness in the other – have been declared by Him who owns a truthful name.

In this way do the charity and merit of laymen grow."

NOTES

Chapter One:

1. Corresponding to Pāli Vesākhā, Sanskrit Vaisākha and Sinhala Vesak.
2. Unlike the Christian Era, the Buddhist Era is reckoned from the death of the Buddha which occurred in 543 B.C.
3. A pillar erected by King Dharmāsōka stands to this day to commemorate the sacred spot.
4. The site of Kapilavatthu has been identified with Bhuila (Bhulya) in the Basti district, three miles from the Bengal and N. W. Railway station of Babuan.
5. See the genealogical table on pp. – 7 & 8
6. Arūpaloka are immaterial planes where those who have developed the Arūpa Jhānas (Absorptions or Ecstasies) are born.
7. Gōtama is the family name, and Sākya is the name of the clan to which the Buddha belonged.

   Traditions hold that the sons of Okkāka of the Mahāsammata line were expelled through the plotting of their stepmother. These princes in the course of their wanderings arrived at the foothills of the Himalayas. Here they met the sage Kapila, on whose advice they founded the city of Kapilavatthu, which they named after him. Hearing of the enterprise of the princes, King Okkāka exclaimed: *"Sākya vata bho, rājakumāra* — Capable indeed are the noble princes."

   Hence the clan and the kingdom they originated were known by the name Sākya.

   The Sākya kingdom was situated in South Nepal and extended over much of modern Oudh.
8. A developed state of consciousness gained by concentration.
9. Also known as Bhaddakaccāna, Bimbā, Rāhulamātā.
10. Kāsi – one of the sixteen Kingdoms of ancient India,

its capital being Benares. It was famous for its silks and perfumes.

11. Māra. According to Buddhism there are five kinds of Māras.
    1. The Five Aggregates (*Khandha*),
    2. Moral and immoral activities (*Abhisamkhāra*),
    3. Death (*Maccu*),
    4. Passion (*Kilesa*) and
    5. Māra the Deity (*Devaputta*).
12. Warriors wear a Munja grass crest on their heads or swords or on their banners to indicate that they will not retreat from the battlefield.
13. As the Buddha attained Enlightenment under the shade of this tree, it was named the Bōdhi Tree. Its descendants are still known by the same name.
14. Buddha is derived from the root budh, to understand. He is called the Buddha because He understood the four Noble Truths. Usually His disciples address their Master as Buddha, *Bhagavā*, etc. When the Buddha refers to Himself He says Tathāgata – Thus who hath come.

Chapter Two

1. Existence
2. i.e. Craving (*Tanhā*)
3. Body
4. Passions
5. Ignorance
6. Nibbāna
7. One who is aspiring to attain Buddhahood is called a *Bōdhisatta* (Bōdhi-Enlightenment; satta-being). This term was applied to Prince Siddhattha before he gained Enlightenment.
8. i.e. from 6 p.m. to 10 p.m.
9. i.e. from 10 p.m. to 2 a.m.
10. On the spot where the Buddha stood, a Caitya has been erected by King Dharmāsōka. This was named Animisalōcana Caitya and is still to be seen.

11. So called because the Buddha reflected on the jewels of the Abhidhamma.
12. These three cannot be passions as this incident took place after the Enlightenment.
13. This Nāga king cannot be a human being. The Vinaya Text also cites an interesting story of a serpent who, assuming the form of a human being, lived for some time as a Bhikkhu in robes.
14. Devatās are celestial or terrestrial deities who, as a rule, are invisible to the naked eye. This particular Devatā had been related to these two merchants in a previous birth.
15. *Cātummahārājikas* – the Guardian Deities of the four Quarters.
16. The Commentary states that the Buddha wished that the four bowls be amalgamated into one.
17. Viz., the Buddha and the Dhamma – *Buddham saranam gacchāmi, Dhammam saranam gacchāmi.* The Sangha or the Noble Order was not in existence then.
    The Jātaka Commentary states that when these two converts begged of the Buddha to give them an object of worship, the Buddha touched His head and presented them some hair.
    It is believed that this particular relic has been enshrined in the modern Shwe Dagon Pagoda in Rangoon.

Chapter Three

1. At first the Buddha did not survey the world with His Divine Eye. He only reflected on the profoundness of the Dhamma which He apprehended.
2. Note the positive term Amata (immortality) which is applied to Nibbāna.
3. The first religious teacher who taught the Bōdhisatta the Jhānas extending to the Realm of Nothingness.
4. The second religious teacher who taught the

Bōdhisatta the highest state of mundane spiritual development – The Realm of Neither Perception nor Non-perception.

5. The tree of Enlightenment
6. The Buddha made such a statement because He attained Enlightenment by Himself without the aid of a teacher. He had teachers before His Enlightenment, but nobody taught Him the way to attain Buddhahood. As such Buddhism is not a natural outgrowth of Hinduism.

Chapter Four

1. Dhammacakka is frequently rendered by "The Wheel of Truth", "The Wheel of Righteousness", "The Kingdom of Righteousness"' etc. According to the commentators Dhamma here means wisdom or knowledge, and cakka means founding or establishment. Dhammacakka, therefore, means the founding or establishment of wisdom, Dhammacakkappavattana means the exposition of the founding of wisdom.
   In this discourse the Buddha expounds the Middle Path which He himself discovered, and which became one of the salient features of His Teaching. He opens the discourse by advising the monks to avoid the two extremes of sensual pleasures and self-mortification. The former retards one's spiritual progress, the latter weakens one's intellect.
2. Modern Sārnāth, where in a former existence the Master sacrificed His life to save a helpless doe and her unborn little one. The locality takes its modern name from the Bōdhisatta who in that ancient birth was Sāranga Nātha, Protector of the Deer.
3. The first extreme was the view of materialists.
4. The five monks along with the ascetics of old adhered to this belief.
5. The Buddha was conversant with both views and

was able to speak of their profitlessness from personal experience. He criticized those views and suggested the most practicable, rational, beneficial path which alone leads to perfect purity and perfect Deliverance.

6. *Rūpa* (Matter), *Vedanā* (sensations), *Saññā* (Perceptions), *Saṁkhāra* (mental states for Volitional Activities) and *Viññāna* (Consciousness).
7. Bhavataṅhā is craving connected with the view of Eternalism Sassata (*Ditthi*).
8. Vibhavatanhā is craving connected with the view of Nihilism Ucchēda (*Ditthi*).
9. i.e. Nibbāna
10. The three aspects are the knowledge of the Truths (*Sacca Ñāna*), the knowledge as regards the function of the Truths (*Kicca Ñāna*), and the knowledge that the function has been accomplished (*Kata Nāna*). Each Truth consists of these three aspects. Thus the four truth consists of twelve modes.
11. He attained Sōtāpatti the first stage of Sainthood. The others attained Sōtāpatti later.

Chapter Five

1. *Dhammacakkhu.* This refers to any of the three lower Paths – Sōtāpatti, Sakadāgāmi, and Anāgāmi.
2. King Seniya Bimbisāra ruled first in Magadha with its capital at Rājagaha. He was the Buddha's first royal patron. Ajātasattu was his ungrateful son. Instigated by Devadatta Thera, he caused the cruel death of his saintly father. Later he became one of the chief lay disciples of the Buddha and took a leading part in the holding of the First Convocation.

Chapter Six

1. *Yamaka Pāthihāriya* – often translated "The Twin Miracle" – is a psychic phenomenon which only

Buddha can perform. By His psychic powers He makes fire and water issue from the pores of the body simultaneously.
2. He saluted Him for the first time when, to his surprise, he saw the infant prince's feet rest on the head of the ascetic Asita whom he wanted the child to revere.

Chapter Seven
1. Abhidhamma is the Highest Doctrine which deals with Buddhist philosophy.
2. That is, since his ordination as a Bhikkhu.

Chapter Eight
1. Late in the evening if He wishes, He takes a bath.

Chapter Nine
1. It was he who rehearsed the Vinaya at the First Council.
2. See Encyclopedia of Religion and Ethics Vol. 7, p. 567; and Prof. T.W. Rhys Davids' Buddhist Birth Stories.

Chapter Ten
1. The Four Iddhipādas are – Will (Chanda), Effort (Viriya), Thought (Citta) and Investigation (Vimamsa).
2. Kappa here means the life-term which was about 100 to 120 years.
3. There are five kinds of Mārās – namely, i. Deity Māra (*Dēvaputta*), ii. Passions (*Kilesa*), iii. Kammic Activities (*Abhisankhāra*), iv. Aggregates (*Khandha*), v. Death (*Maccu*).
4. Sūkaramaddava – According to the Commentary it is tender boar's flesh. Some say it is a kind of mushroom. See Questions of Milinda – Vol. 1. p. 224 and Dialogues of the Buddha Part 2. p. 137.
5. The First Samana is the Sōtāpanna (Stream-Winner), the Second is the Sakadāgāmi (Once-Returner), the

Third is the Anāgāmi (Never-Returner), and the Fourth is the Arahant (Worthy One) who is the Perfect Saint.

6. This Subhadda, the wandering ascetic, should be distinguished from Subhadda who entered the Order in his old age and who remarked that the death of the Buddha was no occasion for sorrow as it left the Bhikkhus free to do whatever they liked without being bound by the injunctions of the Master. That unexpected remark prompted the Venerable Kassapa to take immediate steps to hold a convocation of the Dhamma and Vinaya.
7. The reference was to the Venerable Ānanda who, encouraged by these words, attained Arahantship later.
8. *Jhāna* (Ecstasy or Absorption) is a developed state of mental concentration. Literally it means the burning up of passions or focusing the mind on one object.
9. These are the four Rūpa Jhānas.
10. These are the four Arūpa Jhānas.

Chapter Eleven

1. Abstinence from ten Akusala Kamma is also explained as Kusala Kamma.
2. For details, see the writer's Buddha-Dhamma and The Life of The Buddha and His Teachings.

Chapter Twelve

1. "Christian Heinecken talked within a few hours of his birth at Lubec in 1721, could repeat passages from the Bible at one, answer any question on geography at 2, speak French and Latin at 3, and at 4 years of age was a student of philosophy. He died before he was 5.

   "William James Sidis, wonder child of the United States, could read and write at 2, spoke French, Russian, English, German with some Latin and

Greek at 8, and at 11 lectured on the fourth dimension to a gathering of professors." (The Ceylon Observer, November 21, 1948)
*See Many Mansions and the World Within by Gina Cerminara.

2. "We have come to look upon the present as the child of the past and as the parent of the future." – T.H. Huxley.
3. "It is a strong argument for a state of retribution hereafter that in this world virtuous persons are very often unfortunate and vicious persons prosperous." – Addison..
4. Samsāra – lit. wandering again and again. It is the unbroken process of the Aggregates, Elements and Sense-organs.

Chapter Thirteen

1. See the Dhammacakka Sutta for a brief exposition of the Four Noble Truths. Ch. 4.
2. See Chapter 4.
3. See Chapter 4.

Chapter Fourteen

1. See Bhikhus Silācāra – The Four Noble Truths.
2. *Sa* – with. *Upadi* – aggregates (mind and body), Sesa – remaining. The aggregates are called *Upadi* because they are firmly grasped by craving and false view.

Chapter Fifteen

1. The Eight Precepts are:– Abstaining from: 1. killing, 2. stealing, 3. ignoble conduct (i.e., practising celibacy), 4. lying, 5. intoxicants, 6. taking food after mid-day, 7. dancing, singing, music, unseemly shows, garlands, scents, unguents, 8. high and luxurious seats.
2. The Ten precepts are – The first six are the same as

above. 7. Abstaining from dancing, singing, music and unseemly shows, 8. abstaining from garlands, scents and unguents, 9. abstaining from high and luxurious seats, 10. abstaining from gold and silver (i.e., handling money).

Chapter Seventeen

1. This book was actually compiled by the Venerable Moggaliputta Tissa at the Third Council.
2. All these points pertain to Vinaya discipline. Some of them may not be intelligible to a lay reader.

Chapter Eighteen

1. If 543 B.C. is reckoned as the date of the Parinibbāna of the Buddha, then his coronation must have been in 325 B.C. According to some it is either 270 or 269 B.C.
2. Possibly Nepal was included in the Himalaya region.

Chapter Nineteen

1. Cp. *Mahāmangala Jātaka* (No. 453). This Sutta appears in the Sutta Nipata and Khuddaka Nikāya.
2. Lit., "He who gives alms to the helpless" or "Feeder of the forlorn". His former name was Sudatta. After his conversion to Buddhism, he bought the pleasant grove belonging to Prince Jēta, and erected a monastery which was subsequently named Jētavanā rāma.
   It was in this monastery that the Buddha spent the greater part of His life.
3. Identified with modern Sahet-Mahet on the banks of the Rapti.
4. The Commentary states that one day an interesting discussion arose in the "Public Hall" as to what constituted a Blessing (Mangala). People naturally held diverse views. One declared that auspicious

sights in the early morning (such as a woman with child, little boys, white bulls etc.) should be considered a Mangala; another, auspicious sounds, such as "full", "luck", etc. and yet another, favourable experiences, such as the odour of fragrant flowers, the touching of the earth, etc.

Men were so divided in their opinions that it resulted in the formation of three groups: and this partisanship ultimately extended, so the story goes, even as far as the Deva world. The Devas, who would not rest satisfied until the controversial point was finally settled, appealed to the superior wisdom of their acknowledged leader, Sakka, who, discreet as he was, ordered a certain Deva to approach the Buddha and obtain his trustworthy opinion. It was this particular Deva that drew near the presence of the Blessed One and addressed Him in verse.

5. According to the Commentary "Mangala" means that which is conducive to happiness and prosperity. Etymologists derive the term from three syllables *Mam* (woeful state), ga (going), and la (cut), and is explained as "that which obstructs the way to states of misery."
6. i.e., any place where Bhikkhus, Bhikkhunis, Upāsakas and Upāsikas continually reside, where pious folk are bent on the performance of the ten meritorious deeds, and where the Dhamma exists as a living principle. – Comm.
7. i.e. setting one's immorality in morality, faithlessness in faith, and selfishness in generosity. – Comm.
8. Bahussuta literally means 'much hearing'. This term conveys the same idea as connoted by the word 'erudition' in English. In the ancient days one's education was judged by what one had memorized from oral teaching. Here much learning' refers to knowledge of the Dhamma.

9. The Commentary mentions that handicrafts are of two kinds, namely, the harmless crafts of householders, such as those of the jewellers, goldsmiths, etc. and the crafts of homeless ones, such as stitching of robes, etc.
10. Vinaya, i.e., discipline in thought, word and deed. The Commentary speaks of two kinds of discipline – the discipline of the householder, which is abstinence from the ten immoral actions, and that of the homeless one, which is either the non-transgression of the seven kinds of offences, enumerated in the Pātimokkha, or the observance of the four divisions of Sila (morality).
11. i.e., total abstinence, and not merely temperance.
12. i.e. to Buddha, disciples, teachers, parents, elders, etc. – Comm.
13. For instance, when one is obsessed with evil thoughts – Comm.
14. Those who have calmed their passions.
15. The eight Lōka Dhammas constitute gain and loss, honour and dishonour, praise and blame, happiness and pain.
16. *Asōkam, Virajam* and *Khēmam* – Each of these expressions refers to the mind of the Arahant, Asōka is freedom from sorrow. *Virajam* is freedom from the stains of lust, hatred and ignorance. *Khēmam* is security from the bonds of sense desires (*kāma*), becoming (*bhava*), false views (*ditthi*), and ignorance (*avijja*).
17. i.e., the above-mentioned Thirty-eight Blessings – Comm.
18. Cp. Prof. Rhys Davids' *Buddhism,* p. 125, and Woodward's *Some Sayings of the Buddha,* p. 56.

Chapter Twenty

1. Parābhava (parā + bhava) means downfall.
2. The Devas, who were pleased with the Discourse

on Blessings (the Mangala Sutta) were desirous of hearing the causes of downfall. So a Deva was deputed by them to interrogate the Blessed One.

Chapter Twenty-one

1. As the rainy (Vassāna) season was drawing near, several Bhikkhus received instructions from the Buddha about meditation and went in search of a suitable place. Arriving in the course of their wanderings at a secluded and beautiful spot, they decided to stay there and meditate to gain their Deliverance.

   The Devas, who were dwelling on the tree-tops, resented their presence; and in order to drive them away, disturbed them in their meditation at night. So the Bhikkhus, finding it difficult to concentrate in these circumstances, returned to the Buddha and told Him of their experience.

   Thereupon the Buddha taught them the Sutta of Loving-Kindness, and advised them to go to the same spot and act accordingly.

   The Bhikkhus did so, and now the Devas were pleased at their presence as radiant thoughts of love pervaded the whole atmosphere, and instead of obstructing the spiritual progress of the Bhikkhus, they gave them every possible help.
   Within the Vassāna period itself all the Bhikkhus gained Arahantship.

   This discourse serves both as a mark of protection and as a subject of meditation. In the first part of the discourse are found virtues that should be practiced by anyone who desires one's welfare; in the latter part, the method of practicing Metta or goodwill is explained in detail.
   Metta (Sams. Maitri). It is difficult to give a graceful

English equivalent to this term. Sometimes it is rendered by "benevolence" which is exactly what Metta signifies, but it is too flaccid a word to convey the rapture of Buddhist Metta. See "The Blessing," p. 194.

2. i.e., Nibbāna.
3. *Uju* and *Sūju*. The first term refers to uprightness in word and deed, the second term refers to uprightness in mind – Comm.
4. *Brahma-Vihāra*.
5. Here error means self-illusion (*sakkaāya-ditthi*).
6. i.e. the first glimpse of Nibbāna.
7. When one attains the stage of Anāgāmi, one is born in the Pure Abodes (Suddhāvāsa) and is not born in the human realm.

Chapter Twenty-two

1. The Kōliyans were the rivals of the Sākyans. Queen Mahā Māyā belonged to the Kōliyan clan and King Suddhodana to the Sākyan clan. The Kōliyan capital was at Rāmagāma, about 40 miles east of Kapilavatthu.
2. Literally, long-knee.
3. So called because his ancestors were born on a forest path infested with tigers. Vyagghapajja was Dighajānu's family name.
4. *Saddhā* is not blind faith. It is confidence based on knowledge.
5. *Udumbarakhādakam*. The Commentary explains that one who wishes to eat wood-apple shakes the tree, with the result that many fruits fall but only a few are eaten, whilst a large number is wasted.
6. *Ajaddhumarika – Anathamarana* (Comm.)

CHAPTER 1

1. When was Prince Siddhattha born?
   What is the difference between the Buddhist Era and the Christian Era?
2. Give a brief account of the life of Prince Siddhattha.
3. Mention the chief events connected with the youth of the Prince.
4. What led to the renunciation of Prince Siddhattha?
5. Describe briefly his struggle for Enlightenment.
6. What is the difference between a Bōdhisatta and a Buddha?
7. Mention the three kinds of knowledge developed by the Buddha on the day of His Enlightenment.
8. "The Buddha was neither a saviour nor an incarnation of Vishnu." Comment on this.
9. Was the Buddha a God? Give reasons.
10. "There was none so godlike and so godless as the Buddha." Explain this.
11. "We are all potential Buddhas." Comment on this.
12. Do Buddhists pray to the Buddha to be saved?
13. How did the Buddha serve the world after His Enlightenment?
14. Write notes on:–
    1. Sākyas 2. Asita 3. Kondañña 4. Four Sights 5. Sujāta 6. Uddaka Rāmaputta 7. Mara 8. Māra's army

CHAPTER 2

1. What was the paean of joy the Buddha uttered soon after His Enlightenment?
   What could you infer from this utterance?

2. How did the Buddha spend the first week after His Enlightenment?
3. What was the first moral lesson the Buddha indirectly taught humanity?
4. How does one become a Brahman according to the word of the Buddha?
5. Who were the three daughters of Māra? Could they be passions? Give reasons.
6. What can you say about the sixth week?
7. Give a short account of His first two Converts.
8. What is your opinion about the non-human beings that appear in this chapter? Who were they?
9. How does one formally become a Buddhist? Are there any special ceremonies?
10. Write notes on the following:–
    (i) Mucalinda (ii) Bōdhi tree (iii) Ratana Cankamana (iv) Ratanāghara.

CHAPTER 3

1. Who invited the Buddha to teach, and why?
2. Why was the Buddha reluctant at first to teach the Dhamma though He attained Buddhahood for that very purpose?
3. What was the Buddha's reply to Brahma Sahampati?
4. "No teacher have I." Comment on this.
5. Relate the conversation that took place between the Buddha and Upaka.
6. Give a brief account of the first Five Monks.
7. Describe the meeting of the Buddha with the five monks.

8. Write notes on the following:–
   (i) Brahma Sahampati (ii) Āḷāra Kālāma (iii) Uddakā Rāmaputta (iv) Āvuso (v) Anattalakkhana Sutta.

CHAPTER 4

1. Explain the meaning of "Dhammacakka."
2. What inferences could you draw from the Dhammacakka Sutta?
3. What are the two extremes that should be avoided, and why?
4. Describe the Golden Mean discovered by the Buddha.
5. Give reasons for stating that the Noble Eightfold Path is exclusively Buddhist.
6. Is it necessary to become a Buddhist to follow the Noble Eightfold Path? Give reasons.
7. Explain the Four Noble Truths.
8. Prove that Buddhism is not based on unreasonable belief but on verifiable facts.
9. "Buddhism rests on the pivot of sorrow. Therefore Buddhism is a pessimistic religion." Refute this.
10. How would you account for the problem of suffering?
11. Prove that the world rests on sorrow.
12. Has the second Noble Truth any significance to modern life? Explain.
13. What are the functions of the four Noble Truths?
14. What are the three kinds of craving?
15. Could ultimate Peace be obtained in this present life, and how?
16. Describe the 12 modes of the Four Noble Truths.

17. What happened at the close of this discourse?
18. Prove from this discourse that Buddhism is a moral and philosophical teaching.
19. Craving is a powerful evil force. What good forces have you to summon to subdue this single evil force?
20. Prove from this discourse that the Buddha expounded the doctrine of rebirth.

CHAPTER 5

1. Why did Yasa renounce the world? How did he attain Arahantship?
2. Who were the Buddha's first Upāsaka and Upāsikā?
3. "The Buddha was the First Missioner in the world." Support this statement.
4. Who were the first sixty Arahants?
5. What was the Buddha's exhortation to the first Buddhist missioners?
6. "Seeking oneself is better than seeking others." Comment on this.
7. What is Dhammacakkhu?
8. Give a brief account of the first three ascetics converted by the Buddha.
9. Who was King Bimbisāra and what service did he render to the Sāsana?
10. Describe the conversion of Sāriputta and Moggallāna.
11. Summarise the Buddha's teaching in a few words.
12. Write notes on the following:–
    (i) Ajātasattu (ii) Mahā Nārada Kassapa Jātaka
    (iii) Veluvanārāma (iv) Sanjaya.

CHAPTER 6

1. Describe the Buddha's visit to Kapilavatthu.
2. How did the Buddha convert His relatives?
3. Give a brief account of the conversion of King Suddhōdana.
4. "The Buddha was not a proud aristocrat but a humble mendicant." Comment on this.
5. Describe the Buddha's meeting with Yasōdharā.
6. Who was Nanda, and how was he converted?
7. Give a brief account of the life of Rāhula.
8. Who was the Venerable Ānanda? What special service did he render to women?
9. "Even the Buddha had to face opposition." Comment on this.
10. Does Buddhism advocate vegetarianism or not?

CHAPTER 7

1. Give a brief account of the Order of Nuns.
2. What is Yamaka Pālihāriya? Where did the Buddha exhibit this psychic phenomenon?
3. How did the Buddha pay His gratitude to His mother?
4. Give a brief account of the life of Angulimāla. What lessons do you infer from his life.
5. In whose monastery did the Buddha spend the major part of His life? Give a brief account of his life.
6. What can you say of the chief benefactress of the Buddha? Why is she regarded as an ideal Buddhist lady?
7. Write notes on the following:–

i. Tāvatimsa Heaven
ii. Abhidhamma
iii. Māgandiya
iv. Vēranja
v. Pubbārama
vi. Jetavana.

CHAPTER 8

1. How did the Buddha spend the forenoon session?
2. How many hours a day did the Buddha sleep? How many hours a day did the Buddha preach?
3. In what respects does the Buddha excel other religious teachers?
4. "Buddhism appeals more to the intellect than to emotion." Comment on this.
5. How did the Buddha spend the last watch?

CHAPTER 9

1. "The Buddha was a compassionate and tolerant teacher." Illustrate this.
2. Do you believe that the Buddha was Omniscient? Give reasons.
3. Give an illustration to show that the Buddha did not preach all that He knew.
4. What is the attitude of Buddhism towards caste and nationalism?
5. "The Buddha raised the status of women." Comment on this.
6. "Animals were created for the use of man." Does Buddhism support this statement?
7. What factors have contributed to hail the Buddha as the greatest religious teacher?

CHAPTER 10

1. What did the Buddha say with regard to the four Paths of Accomplishment (*Iddhipāda*)?
2. What part does 'Māra' play in Buddhism?
3. What was the Buddha's exhortation to all His disciples? What were His last words?
4. "He who sees the Dhamma sees me." Comment on this.
5. What was the Buddha's meal? Give reasons for your answer.
6. "The Buddha served humanity up to the last moment." Describe.
7. "The Noble Eightfold Path is found only in Buddhism." Explain this.
8. "All religions lead to the same goal." Refute this.
9. Whom did the Buddha appoint as His successor? Give reasons for His attitude.
10. Describe the last moment of the Buddha.
11. "As a man He was born. As an extraordinary man He lived. As a Buddha He passed away." Comment on this.
12. Write notes on the following:–
    I. Venerable Dhammārāma
    II. Cunda
    III. Subhadda
    IV. The Four Samanas
    V. Jhāna.

CHAPTER 11

1. What is Kamma? What is Vipāka?
2. "Kamma is a law in itself." Explain this.
3. Does Kamma correspond to fate?

4. Explain the difference between Kamma and predestination.
5. What does Kamma explain?
6. "You are your own creator." Comment on this.
7. How does the belief in Kamma affect one's life?
8. "You are born poor on account of your bad Kamma. Do good now to be born rich in your next life." Comment on this.
9. How far does Kamma act as a corrective to man?
10. "Everything is due to Kamma." Refute this.
11. Where is Kamma?
12. Explain the five Niyāmas.
13. If there is no soul, who reaps the effects of Kamma?
14. Write short notes on the different kinds of Kamma.
15. "The doctrine of Kamma is detrimental to the progress of a nation." Refute this.
16. Mention the ten kinds of Kusala Kamma.
17. Describe briefly the ten kinds of evil.
18. Is it wrong to break a fertilized egg? Give reasons.
19. Is transference of merit a Kusala Kamma? Explain how the departed benefit thereby.
20. What are the conditions necessary to complete the evil of killing?
21. Do you abet killing in buying flesh from a meat stall? Give reasons for your answer.
22. Is an action assessed by the motive or by the effect?

CHAPTER 12

1. Explain the difference between rebirth and reincarnation or transmigration.
2. Give your reasons for believing in rebirth.
3. Describe briefly the wheel of life.
4. What are the four modes of birth?
5. How do you account for the unexpected deaths of children?
6. What are the blissful states of existence?
7. How does rebirth take place?
8. If there is no soul, what is it that is reborn? Explain.
9. "Na ca so na ca anno – Neither the same nor another."
   Explain.
10. What do you mean by Pancakkhandha?

CHAPTER 13

1. What is truth?
2. Are the Four Truths dependent or independent of man?
3. Explain the first Noble Truth. Has it any relation to life?
4. What are the Lōkiya and Lōkuttara Truths?
5. Is Buddhism a philosophy, a religion, or an ethical system?

CHAPTER 14

1. What is the meaning of the term Nibbāna?
2. Is Nibbāna nothingness?
3. "There is no difference between the Buddhist Nibbāna and the Christian Heaven." Refute this.

4. What is Sōpādisesa Nibbāna Dhātu?
5. Is Nibbāna attainable in this life itself? Could one realize Nibbāna today?
6. "Nibbāna is supreme bliss." Explain.
7. Explain the difference between Sankhata and Asankhata.
8. Where is Nibbāna?
9. What attains Nibbāna?
10. Is Nibbāna a state or a place?

CHAPTER 15

1. Give in Pali the Noble Eightfold Path.
2. Prove that Buddhism is not based on unreasoning belief.
3. What are Right Thoughts?
4. What is Right Effort?
5. What are the five kinds of prohibited trades?
6. How do you classify the eight factors into three?
7. Give a verse in Pāli which embodies the advice of all the Buddhas.
8. Give a brief description of the first stage that leads to Nibbāna.
9. Is it necessary to enter the Order to attain Nibbāna?
10. What are the Ten Precepts?
11. What are the five kinds of supernormal knowledge?
12. What is Vipassanā?
13. Explain the Three Characteristics (Tilakkhana).
14. Describe briefly the four stages of Sainthood.

15. What are the ten Fetters?
16. How are these Fetters eradicated at different stages?

CHAPTER 16

1. Explain the meaning of the term Nīvarana.
2. Which Hindrance is the most difficult to be eradicated, and why?
3. What is the Buddhist attitude towards repentance?
4. What is Vicikicchā?
5. Mention the five kinds of Hindrances, and explain how they are inhibited and eradicated.

CHAPTER 17

1. Why was a Council held immediately after the passing away of the Buddha?
2. Where and on what date was the First Council held? Who acted as the leading Theras, and why?
3. What is the Tipitaka?
4. Mention the names of five Nikāyas.
5. Give in Pāli the names of the 31 books that comprise the Tipitaka.
6. Mention some of the causes that led to the holding of the Second Council.
7. Mention the names of the leading Theras who participated in the Second council.
8. Who were the chief personages that participated in the Third Council?
9. When was the Third Council held, and why?
10. Has the Third Council any special significance?

CHAPTER 18

1. Give a brief account of the life of Asōka.
2. Who converted Asōka to Buddhism, and how?
3. How did Asōka serve humanity?
4. Disprove that Buddhism was the cause of the downfall of India.
5. Which characteristics of Asōka appeal to you most?
6. Mention the names of the places which Asōka's Missioners visited.
7. Which of these missions was the most successful, and why?
8. Which country preserved the Teaching of the Buddha, and how?

CHAPTER 19

1. Why did the Buddha preach the Mangala Sutta?
2. Give the meaning of the term Mangala.
3. "Buddhism is an other-worldly religion." Refute this with quotations from the Mangala Sutta.
4. Which particular Mangalas contribute to the welfare of a State and why?
5. What Mangalas appeal particularly to children? Give reasons.

CHAPTER 20

1. What is Parābhava, and what led to the preaching of this Sutta?
2. Mention the chief causes that led to the downfall of a boy or a girl?
3. Mention the chief causes that led to the downfall of a man or a woman.

4. Which, in your opinion, are the four chief causes that ruin mankind today?

CHAPTER 21

1. What is the difference between Metta and ordinary love?
2. Mention the virtues that should be practised by a skillful person as stated in the Metta Sutta.
3. What is the criterion of morality according to the Metta Sutta? Comment on it.
4. Describe how Metta should be practised.
5. "A Buddhist is a citizen of the world." Support this statement.

CHAPTER 22

1. Give reasons to show that Buddhism is not an other-worldly religion.
2. What are the four causes that lead to worldly progress?
3. Of these four causes, which is the most important for a boy or a girl?
4. What are the four causes that lead to one's destruction?
5. Mention the four causes that lead to one's spiritual progress?
6. Give in Pāli and English the nine virtues of the Buddha.
7. What is the achievement of virtue?
8. Write notes on the following:–
   (i) *Vyagghapajja*
   (ii) *Saddhā*
   (iii) *Udumbarakhādākam*
   (iv) *Ajaddhumarika*